Herausgegeben von . Edited by

designaustria (DA), Wissenszentrum und Interessenvertretung

Bundesministerium für Wirtschaft, Familie und Jugend

Austria Wirtschaftsservice GmbH

T0312539

Staatspreis Design
2013

**Projekte der Preisträgerinnen
und Preisträger zum Staatspreis Design
& Sonderpreis Design Concepts**
Winning Projects in
the Austrian National Design Prize
& DesignConcepts Award

AMBRA | V

St
p

Staatspreis
Design 2013

des Bundesministeriums
für Wirtschaft, Familie
und Jugend

**Projekte der Preisträgerinnen und Preisträger
zum Staatspreis Design & Sonderpreis Design Concepts**

**Winning Projects in the Austrian National Design Prize
& DesignConcepts Award**

✻ AMBRA | V

Inhalt . Contents

Kreativität und Innovation sind Schlüsselkompetenzen, um im internationalen Wettbewerb erfolgreich bestehen zu können. Design spielt in diesem Zusammenhang eine entscheidende Rolle: Es geht dabei keineswegs nur um die bloße Aufmachung eines Produkts, sondern vielmehr um die Umsetzung von Innovation in die Produktgestaltung. Dadurch trägt Design auch wesentlich zur Entwicklung und Positionierung einer Marke bei, stärkt den Wiedererkennungswert und ist somit ein Instrument zur strategischen Gestaltung des Marktauftritts.

Mit diesem Selbstverständnis wurde heuer zum 45. Mal der Staatspreis Design vergeben. Damit prämiert das Wirtschaftsministerium die besten, kreativsten und innovativsten Designlösungen für Konsumgüter, Investitionsgüter und räumliche Gestaltung.

Die von Designexperten aus dem In- und Ausland ausgezeichneten Produkte werden als Leistungsschau der heimischen Wirtschaft im Rahmen der Verleihungsveranstaltung und mehrerer Ausstellungen präsentiert. Die Preisträger zeigen, dass Österreichs Kreativwirtschaft durch Innovation, Ideenreichtum und Ausdauer wichtige Maßstäbe setzt und damit auf dem richtigen Weg ist. Gleichzeitig wird deutlich, dass die Umsetzung neuester Forschungsergebnisse in materialtechnologischer und mechanischer Hinsicht zunehmend über das Produktdesign erfolgt. An der Schnittstelle zwischen Innovation und Ästhetik ist Design somit ein wichtiger Hebel für wirtschaftlichen Erfolg, dessen Wirkung die prämierten Projekte eindrucksvoll unter Beweis stellen.

Creativity and innovation are key competencies in order to successfully meet the challenges of international competition. In this context, design plays a crucial role: far more is involved here than the mere make-up of a product; rather, design has to do with the implementation of innovation through product development. In this way, design essentially contributes to the growth and positioning of a brand and strengthens its recognition, so that it is an instrument for the strategic evolution of a company's appearance on the market.

With this in mind, the Federal Ministry of Economy has awarded the National Design Prize for the forty-fifth time this year, honouring the best, most creative, and most innovative design solutions for consumer goods, capital goods, and architectural design.

The products, selected by national and international design experts, are to be presented as a performance showcase for Austrian industries, both during the award ceremony and in several exhibitions. The award winners demonstrate that Austria's creative industries set benchmarks through innovation, a wealth of ideas, and persistence and are consequently heading in the right direction. At the same time it becomes obvious that the latest research findings in terms of material technology and mechanics are increasingly translated with the aid of product design. An interface between innovation and aesthetics, design is thus a major leverage for economic success whose impact is impressively evidenced by the award-winning projects.

Dr. Reinhold Mitterlehener
Bundesminister für Wirtschaft, Familie und Jugend
Federal Minister of Economy, Family and Youth

bmw fi
Bundesministerium für
Wirtschaft, Familie und Jugend

Von der Unzufriedenheit zur Innovation
Zur Ausschreibung des Sonderpreises DesignConcepts

Als Förderbank der Republik Österreich hat die Austria Wirtschaftsservice GmbH (aws) insbesondere auch die Aufgabe, in die Innovationskraft der österreichischen Wirtschaft zu investieren. Gerade im Bereich der Kreativwirtschaft gilt es dabei zunächst, sich mit den Motiven und Bedürfnissen der Akteure auseinanderzusetzen. »Unzufriedenheit« ist meistens die Antwort auf die Frage, was Designerinnen und Designer antreibt. Keine »raunzende« und »antriebslose« Unzufriedenheit, sondern eine Unzufriedenheit mit Mittelmaß, Scheinlösungen und Stillstand, geäußert aus der Perspektive des Verändern-Wollens.

»Es geht auch anders!« betonen immer wieder die Vertreterinnen und Vertreter der Kreativwirtschaft. Doch ehe »das Andere« sich als »besser« erweist und ehe sich ihre Ideen als Impulse wirtschaftlicher und gesellschaftlicher Weiterentwicklung entpuppen, warten unbelohntes Tüfteln und zahlreiche Sackgassen unter dem Damoklesschwert des Scheiterns.

Das Förderprogramm »impulse« der aws trägt als Teil der Kreativwirtschaftsinitiative »evolve« des Bundesministeriums für Wirtschaft, Familie und Jugend die Risiken und Nebenwirkungen des »Anders« mit. Von der finanziellen Unterstützung, den Awareness- und Weiterbildungsmaßnahmen profitieren auch jene Designer und Designerinnen, die zunächst die Tauglichkeit ihrer Konzepte erkunden müssen, bis sie imstande sind, ausgereifte Lösungen am Markt feilzubieten. »impulse« I aws begleitet unternehmerisch denkende Kreative von der Idee bis zum Markterfolg.

In diesem Kontext liegt es nahe, dass »impulse« I aws in Kooperation mit dem Wirtschaftsministerium wieder den Sonderpreis DesignConcepts stiftet. Er zeichnet bislang noch nicht umgesetzte, innovative Konzepte mit hohem Marktpotenzial aus. Junge Designerinnen und Designer soll der Preis ermutigen, ihre Kreativität in unternehmerische Bahnen zu lenken und dem Wirtschaftsstandort Österreich die notwendigen Innovationsschübe zu verpassen.

From Dissatisfaction to Innovation
The Calls for the DesignConcepts Award

As the Austrian government promotional bank, the Austria Wirtschaftsservice GmbH (aws) particularly also has the responsibility of investing in the innovative strength of the Austrian economy. As far as the creative industries sector is concerned, the first step is to explore the motives and needs of the players involved. If one looks for the answer to the question of what the driving force behind designers is, one is quickly confronted with the word »dissatisfaction«: not a »grumbling« and »unmotivated« sort of dissatisfaction, but a dissatisfaction with sham solutions, mediocrity, and stagnation that is expressed out of a desire to make changes.

»There's a different way!« the representatives of the creative industries emphasize time and again. But before their ideas turn out to be stimuli for economic and social progress, before »different« proves to be »better«, failure hangs like the Sword of Damocles over unrewarded, meticulous work and innumerable dead ends.

The »impulse« promotion programme launched by aws as part of the Federal Ministry of Economy, Family and Youth's »evolve« initiative for the creative industries helps bear the risks and fall-out of being »different«. Those designers who must first investigate the feasibility of their concepts until they are in a position to put fully developed solutions for sale on the market also profit from the financial support, the advanced training, and the awareness opportunities being offered.

In this context, it is obvious that »impulse« | aws, in conjunction with the Federal Ministry of Economy, Family and Youth, again endows the DesignConcepts Award. It is granted for innovative concepts with a high market potential that have not yet been implemented. The prize is intended to encourage young designers to direct their creativity into business avenues and to give Austria as a business location the innovative nudge it needs.

DI Bernhard Sagmeister
Geschäftsführer Austria Wirtschaftservice GmbH
Managing Director Austria Wirtschaftsservice GmbH

Zum Staatspreis Design
& Sonderpreis DesignConcepts 2013

Vor allem in der Kategorie Konsumgüter war die Jury mit einer solchen Bandbreite an Einreichungen – vom Kinderspielzeug bis zum Automobil – konfrontiert, dass der Wunsch laut wurde, die Produkte nach Möglichkeit auch im Original zu begutachten. Befürwortet wurde diese durchaus nachvollziehbare Anregung von den erfahrenen Designprofis Fritz Frenkler und Gerald Kiska. Der eine ist Partner eines Designbüros in München, das seine Fühler auch, aber nicht nur nach Japan ausstreckt, und steht dem Lehrstuhl für Industrial Design an der Fakultät für Architektur der Technischen Universität München (TUM) vor, der andere ist Begründer und Leiter eines der größten eigentümergeführten Designstudios Europas, mit Sitz in Salzburg. Beiden geht es um eine ganzheitliche, glaubwürdige und der Funktion angemessene Produktsprache und -kommunikation, die sie auch dem Designnachwuchs vermitteln. Der Ausbildung von Designern widmet sich mit großem Engagement auch Günther Grall, Leiter und Professor des Studiengangs Design und Produktmanagement an der Fachhochschule Salzburg, der mit seinen Studierenden vor allem im Bereich Möbeldesign neue Lösungen auslotet. Möbelbranche und Holzbau sind auch die Domänen der ausgebildeten Medien- und Designexpertin Karin Polzhofer, die Marketingleiterin des eigenen designorientierten Familienunternehmens ist und sich mit Leidenschaft für gute Gestaltung einsetzt. Als zweiter Vertreter der österreichischen Wirtschaft hatte Johannes Scheuringer, einer der Geschäftsführer eines vielfach ausgezeichneten oberösterreichischen Fenster- und Türenbauers, ein Auge auf eine markt- und markentaugliche Umsetzung von Designinnovation. Den geladenen Jurorinnen und Juroren standen Stefanie Grüssl vom Bundesministerium für Wirtschaft, Familie und Jugend sowie – in beratender Funktion – »impulse«-Programmleiterin Sabine Pümpel von der Austria Wirtschaftsservice GmbH zur Seite. Alle Mitglieder der Jury werden am Ende des Katalogs in Wort und Bild vorgestellt.

Insgesamt lagen der Jury 166 Einreichungen von 112 Teilnehmern vor, was in etwa dem Zulauf des Vorbewerbs entspricht und angesichts der schwierigen Wirtschaftslage die Erwartungen übertraf. Positiv ist zu vermerken, dass es im Bereich Produktgestaltung sowohl bei den Konsumgütern (70 gegenüber 58) als auch bei den Investitionsgütern (40 gegenüber 30) signifikante Zuwächse gab; leichte Rückgänge waren in der räumlichen Gestaltung zu verzeichnen (22 gegenüber 30). Dass in der Konzeptkategorie, wo es um noch nicht realisierte Gestaltungslösungen geht, die Anzahl der Beiträge beinahe um die Hälfte zurückgegangen ist (34 gegenüber 62), ist wohl auf die prekäre Situation von Jungunternehmern und Neugründern in der Kreativbranche zurückzuführen. Obwohl sich zahlreiche führende österreichische Wirtschaftsunternehmen und Designstudios an der größten Leistungsschau des Landes für dreidimensionale Gestaltung beteiligt haben, steht, wie auch die Mitglieder der Jury angemerkt haben, zu hoffen, dass beim nächsten Mal noch mehr ausgezeichnete Projekte für eine Teilnahme gewonnen werden können. Es geht darum, den Staatspreis Design als auch international wahrgenommenes Schaufenster zu nützen und Österreichs Kompetenz in Sachen Design, Innovation und Herstellungsqualität ins Schweinwerferlicht zu stellen.

Licht war übrigens ein großes Thema in allen Kategorien, von der Produkt- bis hin zur räumlichen Gestaltung und zu den Designkonzepten: In der Shortlist finden sich Lichtlösungen für den Wohn- und Arbeitsbereich, eine Straßenleuchte, ein neues Beleuchtungssystem für ein historisches Hallenbad sowie eine High-Tech-Jacke, die Radfahrer bei Dunkelheit sichtbar macht. Sie alle basieren auf neuesten technologischen Standards. Die insgesamt 24 ausgewählten und in diesem Katalog vorgestellten Projekte zeichnen sich durch soziale Relevanz aus und werden einem modernen Lebensstil gerecht, der sich durch technisch und gestalterisch

komplexe, aber bedienerfreundliche und funktionale Lösungen sowie hochwertige Materialien besser verwirklichen lässt als durch oberflächliche Behübschung. Die Jury hat in den Hauptkategorien acht von neun möglichen Nominierungen und in der Folge alle drei Staatspreise vergeben. Bei den Konsumgütern findet sich ein breites Spektrum unterschiedlicher Produkte, die den Lebensalltag erleichtern oder angenehm gestalten, angeführt von einem elektronisch gesteuerten Beinprothesensystem, das an die Perfektion des menschlichen Kniegelenks herankommt. Bei den Investitionsgütern stehen eine Verbesserung der Arbeitswelt und eine Aufwertung des Arbeitsplatzes im Vordergrund, bei der räumlichen Gestaltung die Verbindung von Historie und zeitgenössischer Architektur. Erfreulich ist, dass sich unter den ausgewählten Beiträgen auch internationale Kooperationen mit Deutschland, Italien und Liechtenstein befinden. In der Sonderkategorie DesignConcepts kamen der mit 5.000 Euro dotierte Hauptpreis sowie zwei mit 3.000 beziehungsweise 2.000 Euro dotierte Anerkennungspreise zur Vergabe. Gleich zwei Geldpreise vergab die Jury einstimmig an Konzepte, die sich mit der Integration neuer Medien in den Schulunterricht beschäftigen.

Wir danken allen Teilnehmerinnen und Teilnehmern für ihre Bereitschaft, sich mit ihren Produkten und Gestaltungslösungen einer unabhängigen Fachjury zu stellen. Sie haben damit einen wichtigen Beitrag geleistet, österreichisches Design sichtbar zu machen. Herzliche Gratulation den Gewinnerinnen und Gewinnern!

The National Design Prize & The DesignConcepts Award 2013

Above all in the category of consumer goods, the jury was confronted with such a diverse array of entries – from a child's toy to an automobile – that the wish was expressed to be able to judge the products in the original. This entirely understandable proposal was primarily advocated by the experienced design professionals Fritz Frenkler and Gerald Kiska: the first holds the chair for industrial design in the Department of Architecture at the Munich University of Technology (TUM) and is a partner in a design office in Munich that has extended its reach as far as Japan; the second is the founder and CEO of one of Europe's largest owner-managed design studios, located in Salzburg. Both of them favour a holistic, credible, and functionally appropriate product language and communication, which they also seek to convey to future generations of designers. Günther Grall, head and professor of the design and product management master's course at the Salzburg University of Applied Sciences, also ardently commits himself to the training of design youngsters. With his students, he explores first and foremost new solutions in the field of furniture design. Wood construction and the furniture industry are also the domains of media and design expert Karin Polzhofer, who now is marketing director of her own design-oriented family enterprise and passionately devotes herself to good design. As a second representative of the Austrian business world, Johannes Scheuringer, one of the CEOs of a widely acclaimed Upper Austrian manufacturer of windows and doors, kept an eye out for the implementation of design innovation conducive to marketability and brand enhancement. The invited jurors were supported by Stefanie Grüssl of the Federal Ministry of Economy, Family and Youth and Sabine Pümpel, manager of the »impulse« programme of the Austria Wirtschaftsservice GmbH, who contributed to the decision-making process in an advisory role. All of the members of the jury are introduced in words and pictures at the end of this catalogue.

The jury had to assess a total of 166 submissions from 112 entrants, which approximately corresponds to the participation in the contest's previous edition and, in the face of the difficult economic situation, exceeded the organizers' expectations. A significant increase in both product design categories – in consumer goods (70 compared to 58) and capital goods (40 compared to 30) – was observed as a positive trend, whereas a minor decrease was registered in the architectural design category (22 compared to 30). That the number of contributions fell by almost half in the design concepts category (34 compared to 62), which involves design solutions not yet marketed, is probably related to the precarious situation of young entrepreneurs and start-ups in the creative industries. Although a large number of the country's leading commercial enterprises and design studios took part in Austria's major performance show for three-dimensional design, the organizers hope that next time even more outstanding projects will be submitted – a wish that was also expressed by the members of the jury. It is crucial to make use of the National Design Prize as a showcase that also attracts international attention and to spotlight Austria's competencies in design, innovation, and production quality.

Light was, by the way, a prominent subject in all of the categories, from product design to architectural design and design concepts: the shortlisted entries include light solutions for domestic and office environments, a streetlight, a new lighting concept for a historical indoor swimming pool, and a high-tech jacket that makes cyclists visible in the dark, all of which are based on state-of-the-art technological standards. The altogether 24 selected projects presented in this catalogue are characterized by social relevance and do justice to a modern lifestyle that can certainly be realized more effectively through solutions advanced in terms of technology, material, and design, yet user friendly and highly functional, than through superficial embellishment. In the main categories, the jury awarded eight out of nine possible nominations and subsequently all of the three National Design Prizes. In the consumer goods category is a large spectrum of products whose focus is on making everyday life easier or more convenient, with an electronically controlled leg prosthetic system approximating the perfection of the human knee joint leading the way. Many of the winning entries in the capital goods category are aimed at improving job environments and enhancing the workplace, while several architectural design projects concentrate on a successful combination of history and contemporary architecture. And it is remarkable that the final selection also includes international collaborative efforts – with companies in Germany, Italy, and Liechtenstein. In the DesignConcepts category, all of the available funds were distributed: the main prize, in the amount of 5,000 euros, as well as two distinctions, at 3,000 and 2,000 euros respectively. As many as two of these cash prizes were unanimously awarded for concepts promoting the integration of new media into school education.

We would like to extend our thanks to all of the participants for their willingness to submit their products and design solutions to the judgement of an independent jury of experts and for having thereby contributed to making Austrian design visible. Our congratulations to the winners!

Jurybericht
Jury Report

Staatspreis Design
Produktgestaltung | Industrial Design –
Konsumgüter
National Design Prize
Product Design | Industrial Design –
Consumer Goods

Genium
Beinprothesensystem

Das Design der Prothese berücksichtigt, dass
dieses Produkt Menschen dient, die sich in einer
Ausnahmesituation befinden. Die formale Ausge-
glichenheit und der Umgang mit der Technik tragen
hier zu einer Entstigmatisierung bei und bieten
eine Alternative an, welche die Würde des Trägers
wahrt. Trotzdem es sich um ein hochtechnisches
Produkt handelt, wurde hier mit großer Behutsam-
keit vorgegangen. Gestalter und Ingenieure waren
sich der Tatsache bewusst, dass ihre Entwicklung
einen menschlichen Körperteil ersetzen soll. Die
solide Konstruktion strahlt Sicherheit aus und
erweckt Vertrauen. Die Verbindung von Technik,
Robustheit und zurückhaltender und dennoch
selbstbewusster Ästhetik überzeugt formal wie
funktional.

Genium
Prosthetic leg system

The design for this prothesis takes into account
that the product serves individuals coping in an
exceptional situation. The formal balance and superior handling of technology contribute to destig-
matization and offer an alternative that preserves
the amputee's dignity. Although this is a high-tech
product, it was approached with great sensitivity.
The designers and engineers certainly were aware
that their development was to replace a part of
the human body. The solid construction emanates
safety and fosters a sense of trust. The combination of technology, robustness, and a cautious,
yet self-confident aesthetic appeal proves convincing in terms of both form and function.

Staatspreis Design
Produktgestaltung | Industrial Design –
Investitionsgüter
National Design Prize
Product Design | Industrial Design –
Capital Goods

Einsatzschiff der Schiffsaufsicht des
Bundesministeriums für Verkehr,
Innovation und Technologie

Die moderne, saubere und zweckmäßige Gestaltung dieses Wasserfahrzeugs entspricht seiner
Funktion als Arbeitsboot und ist somit dem
Produkt ganz und gar angemessen. Das Design ist
solide, aber nicht betont industriell. Es berücksichtigt, dass Menschen hier einer beruflichen Tätigkeit
nachgehen und stellt somit eine Würdigung und
Aufwertung ihrer Arbeit dar. Entsprechend ist im
Inneren des Schiffes auch ein großzügiger Sozial-
bereich vorgesehen. Der Verzicht auf Überflüssiges
und der nachvollziehbare Aufbau erleichtern War-
tung und Reinigung. Mit seinem klaren, kristallinen
Körper hat das Dienstboot nicht nur einen starken
Auftritt, sondern vermittelt auch von außen einen
schönen Eindruck.

Utility Boat for the River Police
of the Federal Ministry for Transport,
Innovation and Technology

The modern, clean, and practical design of this watercraft complies with its function as a utility boat
and is therefore absolutely appropriate. It looks
solid, but not overly industrial. The solution takes
into consideration that this is a working environment. Its high quality honours the work that is per-
formed here and elevates it. Accordingly, the vessel
is also furnished with generous community space.
The renouncement of superfluous embellishment
and the well-thought-out structure facilitate maintenance and cleaning. With its clear, crystalline
body, this patrol boat is not only impressive, but
also beautiful to look at.

Staatspreis Design
Räumliche Gestaltung
National Design Prize
Architectural Design

Neuer Salzburger Hauptbahnhof

Hier überzeugt die Gestaltung im Ganzen und im Detail. Historisch wichtige Teile wurden erhalten und mit neuen, modernen Materialien und Formen zusammengeführt. Das Projekt zeichnet sich einerseits durch einen respektvollen Umgang mit der vorhandenen Bausubstanz aus, zum anderen kommen neue Technologien und eine minimalistische und puristische Formensprache zum Zug, die das Bauwerk in seinem Erscheinungsbild und in seiner Funktion für die Zukunft tragfähig machen. Historie und eine »Zweite Moderne« verbinden sich hier zu einer durch und durch gelungenen Einheit.

New Salzburg Central Station

The design of this building makes a great impact both as a whole and in detail. Historically relevant parts have been preserved and combined with new, modern forms and materials. On the one hand, the project stands out for the designers' respectful approach to the extant substance; on the other hand, new technologies and a minimalist and purist language of form make themselves clearly felt and ensure the structure's sustainability for the future in terms of both function and appearance. Here history and a »Second Modernity« merge to create a thoroughly satisfactory union.

Sonderpreis DesignConcepts
DesignConcepts Award

EDU Spind
Kommunikationssystem für Schulen

Dieses einfache, kostengünstige und sofort umsetzbare System ist modular, verstellbar und flexibel und bietet eine charmante wie notwendige Lösung für den Schulalltag. Der Spind dient als Ladestation für elektronische Geräte, privater Stauraum und Briefkasten. Mit seinen vielfältigen Funktionen bietet er sowohl für die Nutzer (die Schüler) als auch für den Provider (die Schule) einen Mehrwert. Trotzdem das System auf einem Massenprodukt – sozusagen auf einem Readymade – aufbaut, ist es gestalterisch schön und überzeugend interpretiert.

EDU Locker
Communication system for schools

This simple, inexpensive system, which offers a charming and essential solution for day-to-day school life, is variable, adaptable, flexible, and immediately practicable. The locker serves as a charging station for electronic devices, a private storage unit, and a mailbox. Thanks to its multiple functions it offers added value for both users (the students) and the provider (the school). Although the system is based on a mass product – a ready-made, so to speak – it has been beautifully designed and convincingly interpreted.

DesignConcepts
Anerkennungspreis
DesignConcepts
Distinction

EDU Buch
Integration neuer Medien
in den Schulalltag

Handy und Schule sind kein Widerspruch: Hier wird
das Smartphone als Tool in den Unterricht integriert und muss nicht vom Lehrpersonal konfisziert
werden, weil es einer in der Schulstunde nicht
vorgesehenen Nutzung zugeführt wird. Letztend-
lich ersetzt es sogar den Schulranzen. Dank der
entsprechenden Technologie und Software trägt
diese Lösung zu einer Einheit von analogem und
digitalem Lernen bei.

EDU Book
Integration of new media into everyday
school life

Mobile phones and school are not necessarily
adversaries: this concept allows smartphones to be
integrated into lessons, eliminating the need for
teachers to confiscate them for having been used
inappropriately. Ultimately this concept can even
replace schoolbags. Thanks to pertinent technology and software, this solution contributes to
uniting analogue and digital learning.

DesignConcepts
Anerkennungspreis
DesignConcepts
Distinction

Fred/Fold
Klappbike

Dieses vollwertige Fahrrad lässt sich dank der spe-
ziellen Drehachse mit einem einfachen Handgriff
auf 40 Prozent seines Volumens reduzieren und
passt daher in jeden Kofferraum. Das zum Einsatz
kommende Material Karbon macht es zudem zu
einem Leichtgewicht. Damit erfüllt das Produkt
in zweifacher Hinsicht zeitgemäße Ansprüche, die
nicht nur im Hinblick auf die Funktion, sondern
auch gestalterisch plausibel umgesetzt wurden.

Fred/Fold
Folding bike

Thanks to a specially constructed pivot axle, this
fully fledged bicycle can effortlessly be reduced
to 40 per cent of its volume, so that it fits into any
car boot. In addition, carbon is employed to make
this vehicle particularly lightweight. Consequently,
the product meets contemporary requirements in a
twofold way, not only with regard to function, but
also in terms of a convincing design.

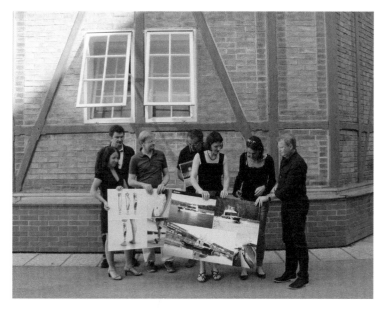

Tèo
Löffel zur Bereitung von Tee
Spoon for preparing tea
Design
Lucy.D

Helios
LED-Leuchten
LED lights
Design
Kai Stania | Product Design

Genium
Beinprothesensystem
Prosthetic leg system
Design
Studio Novo Communication
& Product Design e.U.

consistent design r117
TV-Receiver und Fernbedienung
TV set-top box and remote control
Design
zeug design gmbh

Produktgestaltung
Product Design

Industrial Design
Industrial Design

Konsumgüter
Consumer Goods

Lentia
Stuhl
Chair
Design
March Gut Industrial Design

Majestic –
Woodstone Collection
Stein-Holz-Brillenfassung
Stone-and-wood spectacle frame
Design
ROLF Spectacles

Inipi B
Kompaktsauna
Compact sauna
Design
EOOS

Pandoretta
360° Wireless Audio System
Design
Thomas Feichtner

Produktgestaltung | Industrial Design
Konsumgüter
Staatspreis Design
**Product Design | Industrial Design
Consumer Goods**
National Design Prize

Genium

Beinprothesensystem . Prosthetic leg system

**Design
Studio Novo Communication
& Product Design e. U.**
Neubaugasse 59/2/2
A-1070 Wien
T +43 (0)1 890 20 97
E info@studio-novo.com
www.studio-novo.com

**Auftraggeber & Produzent
Client & Producer
Otto Bock Healthcare GmbH**
Kaiserstraße 39
A-1070 Wien
T +43 (0)1 523 37 86
E info.austria@ottobock.com
www.ottobock.at

Dass man die Perfektion des menschlichen Knie-gelenks nur annähernd erreichen kann, macht ein Projekt wie dieses zur Herausforderung. Die schlanke Linienführung orientiert sich an der Anatomie des Unterschenkels und verleiht der mikroprozessorgesteuerten Prothese einen selbst-bewussten Auftritt. Das intuitive System unter-stützt den natürlichen Bewegungsablauf, ohne dass der Träger das Gelenk bewusst steuern muss, und reagiert intelligent auf Alltagssituationen. Messsensoren überprüfen permanent, in welcher Phase des Gehens man sich befindet, wodurch sich der bewusste Kraft und Koordinationsauf wand deutlich reduziert. Auch Treppensteigen im Wechselschritt ist möglich. Weitere Vorteile sind die induktive Ladung, eine lange Akkulaufzeit und Spritzwasserbeständigkeit.

That the perfection of the human knee joint can only be roughly approximated makes projects like this a particular challenge. The slender outlines, lending the microprocessor-controlled prosthesis a self-confident appearance, mimic the anatomy of the lower leg. The intuitive system, which responds intelligently to everyday situations, supports natural movement and spares the wearer the need to wilfully control the joint. Measuring sensors constantly monitor each phase of walking so that the wearer's conscious effort in terms of strain and coordination is considerably reduced. Therefore it is also possible to ascend and descend stairs step over step. Further benefits include inductive charging, extended battery life, and resistance to splash water.

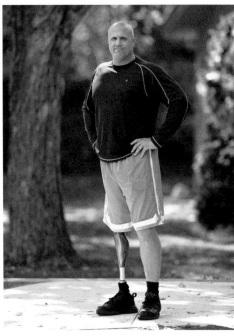

Produktgestaltung | Industrial Design
Konsumgüter
Nominierung
Product Design | Industrial Design
Consumer Goods
Nomination

Tèo

Löffel zur Bereitung von Tee . Spoon for preparing tea

Design
Lucy.D
Barbara Ambrosz, Karin Santorso
Halbgasse 20/3
A-1070 Wien
T +43 (0)676 550 70 89
E office@lucyd.com
www.lucyd.com

Auftraggeber & Produzent
Client & Producer
Alessi S.p.A.
Via privata Alessi
I-28887 Crusinallo di Omegna
E progetti.alessi@alessi.com
www.alessi.com

Dieser elegante Edelstahllöffel macht Teetrinken auch dann zum entspannten Ritual, wenn Tee im Beutel zubereitet wird. Der Beutel, dessen Faden innerhalb des hohlen Löffelstiels verläuft, kommt samt Löffel in den Tee und wird durch das Etikett am Ende des Fadens fixiert. Nach der Infusionszeit zieht der Teetrinker den Beutel durch den Stiel und drückt ihn damit aus, ohne dass seine Geschicklichkeit herausgefordert wird. Die verbliebene Flüssigkeit läuft in die Tasse zurück. Der Umgang mit dem Produkt, das durch seine Einfachheit und Funktionalität besticht, ist unkompliziert und leicht in den Alltag integrierbar, egal ob Zuhause oder im Büro.

This elegant stainless steel spoon ensures that drinking tea remains a relaxing ritual even if teabags are used. The teabag, whose thread runs inside the hollow handle, is held in place by the label at the end of the thread and is lowered into the mug or cup together with the spoon. Once the tea has steeped, the bag is gently squeezed out by comfortably pulling it through the handle. The excess liquid flows back into the cup. This product, which is charming because of its simplicity and functionality, is uncomplicated to use and can easily be integrated into daily routines, whether at home or at work.

Produktgestaltung | Industrial Design
Konsumgüter
Nominierung
Product Design | Industrial Design
Consumer Goods
Nomination

consistent design r117

TV-Receiver und Fernbedienung . TV set-top box and remote control

Design
zeug design gmbh
Detlev Magerer, Erwin Weitgasser
Morzger Straße 4
A-5020 Salzburg
T +43 (0)662 8355 20-0
E office@zeug.at
www.zeug.at

Auftraggeber & Produzent
Client & Producer
ruwido austria gmbh
Köstendorfer Straße 8
A-5202 Neumarkt a. W.
T +43 (0)6216 4571-0
E sales@ruwido.com
www.ruwido.com

Das Konzept basiert auf einem ganzheitlichen Ansatz für Fernbedienung und Receiver. Die Formensprache des Geräts, das von einem CNC-gefrästen Vollaluminiumgehäuse ummantelt wird, erlaubt die Integration multimodaler Funktionen. Beim Scrollen durch Programme und Sender liefert ein patentiertes Steuerungs- und Eingabesystem, das sich dynamisch am Nutzer orientiert, haptisches Feedback. Die Verwendung von Sprache als zusätzliches Navigationselement reduziert die erforderliche Anzahl der Tasten auf ein Minimum und sorgt für ein klares Erscheinungsbild. Sprachübertragung in HI-FI-Qualität ermöglicht nicht nur die direkte Suche nach TV-Inhalten, sondern auch Sprachidentifikation und -erkennung. Ästhetik, hochwertige Materialität, intuitive Navigation und Produktintelligenz liefern starke Anwendererlebnisse.

This concept is based on a holistic design approach to a remote control and set-top box. The formal vocabulary of the device, which is surrounded by a CNC-milled aluminium case, allows for the integration of multimodal functions. When scrolling through the programmes and stations, a patented control and input system dynamically adapting to the user offers tactile feedback. Using voice control as an additional element for navigation reduces the required number of buttons to a minimum and enhances visual clarity. Voice transmission in hi-fi quality not only makes it possible to search directly for TV contents, but also provides for voice identification and recognition. The product's aesthetic appeal, high-quality material, intuitive navigation, and intelligence deliver an impressive user experience.

**Produktgestaltung | Industrial Design
Konsumgüter**
Design ausgewählt
**Product Design | Industrial Design
Consumer Goods**
Honourable Mention

Helios

LED-Leuchten . LED lights

**Design
Kai Stania | Product Design**
Hühnersteigstraße 71
A-1140 Wien
T +43 (0)664 104 66 11
E office@kaistania.com
www.kaistania.com

**Auftraggeber & Produzent
Client & Producer
XAL GmbH**
Auer-Welsbach-Gasse 36
A-8055 Graz
T +43 (0)316 3170
E office@xal.com
www.xal.com

Neue Arbeitsformen und Technologien erfordern adäquate Lichtlösungen. Schon die Silhouette des reduzierten Aluminiumrahmens steht – sowohl bei der Deckenleuchte als auch bei der universell einsetzbaren Stehleuchte – für Klarheit, sodass die innovative LED-Technologie voll und ganz zur Geltung kommen kann. Das Licht der dimmbaren LEDs strahlt in die obere Plexiglasscheibe, die es horizontal und vertikal verteilt (LGP/light guiding prism), während es die untere Plexiglasscheibe diffus nach unten streut (CPL/circular prismatic layer). In ausgeschaltetem Zustand wird der minimalistische Rahmen kaum wahrgenommen. Ein magischer Moment entsteht, wenn die durchsichtigen Scheiben beim Einschalten zu einer Leuchtfläche werden und die Lampe selbst ganz in den Hintergrund tritt.

New work situations and technologies require adequate lighting solutions. In the case of both the ceiling light and the universally applicable floor lamp, the silhouette of the reduced aluminium frame alone radiates clarity and thus offers a perfect setting for the innovative LED technology to come into its own. The dimmable LEDs direct the light into the upper Perspex disk, which distributes it horizontally and vertically (LGP/light guiding prism), whereas the lower Perspex disk diffusely disperses the light downwards (CPL/circular prismatic layer). When the light is turned off, the minimalist frame is hardly discernable. A magic moment occurs when the transparent disks are transformed into illuminated surfaces as soon as the light is turned on, whereas the lamp as such is entirely eclipsed.

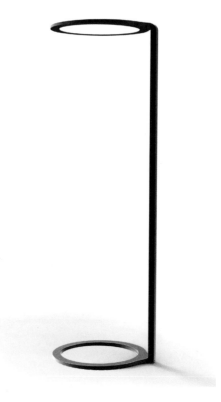

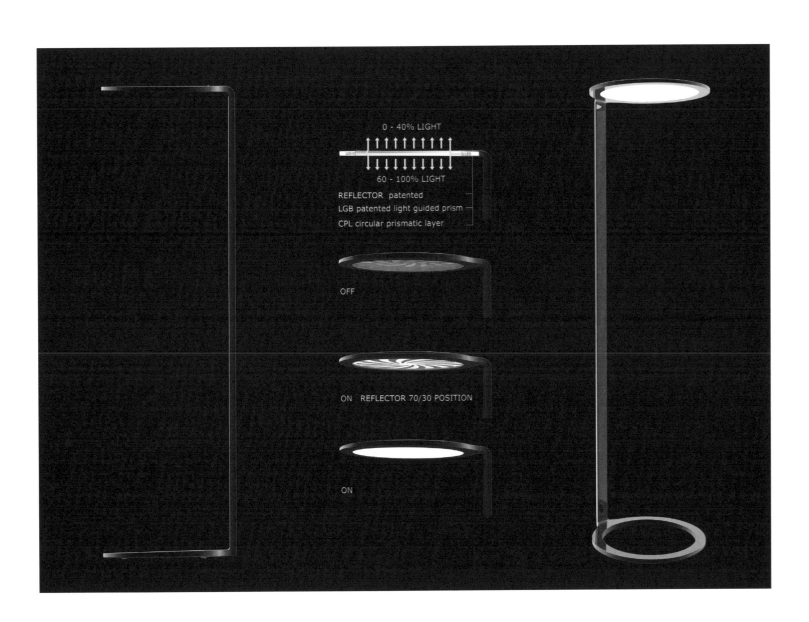

0 - 40% LIGHT

60 - 100% LIGHT

REFLECTOR patented

LGB patented light guided prism

CPL circular prismatic layer

OFF

ON   REFLECTOR 70/30 POSITION

ON

**Produktgestaltung | Industrial Design
Konsumgüter**
Design ausgewählt
**Product Design | Industrial Design
Consumer Goods**
Honourable Mention

Lentia

Stuhl . Chair

**Design
March Gut Industrial Design**
Tummelplatz 1
A-4020 Linz
T +43 (0)732 772 839-13
E studio@marchgut.com
www.marchgut.com

**Auftraggeber & Produzent
Client & Producer
Pühringer GmbH & Co KG**
Böhmdorf 7b
A-4193 Reichenthal
T +43 (0)7214 4232
E office@puehringer.com
www.puehringer.com

Dieser Stuhl verschreibt sich eher der Leichtig-keit des Seins, als dass der einem exzentrischen Lebensstil frönt. Die Sitz- und Lehnflächen aus schichtverleimtem Holz ruhen auf stabilen Massivholzbeinen. Die sich an die Basis schmie-genden Bugholzflächen sorgen für optimalen Sitzkomfort. Das Resultat ist ein Produkt, das in Form und Gewicht ausgewogen ist und in dem sich die Traditionen des klassischen Stuhlbaus mit zeitgenössischer Gestaltung verbinden. Trotz seiner leichtgewichtigen Anmutung strahlt dieses Sitz-möbel eine tiefe Verwurzelung aus.

This chair is devoted to the lightness of being rather than to encouraging an extravagant lifestyle. The laminated wood seat and resting parts are supported on stable solid wood legs, with the bentwood parts nestling against the base and providing optimal seating comfort. The result is a product ideally balanced in its form and weight in which the traditions of classic chairmaking ideally coincide with contemporary design. Despite its lightweight appearance, this piece of seating furniture makes a profoundly rooted impression.

Produktgestaltung | Industrial Design
Konsumgüter
Design ausgewählt
Product Design | Industrial Design
Consumer Goods
Honourable Mention

Design
EOOS
Zelinkagasse 2/6
A-1010 Wien
T +43 (0)1 405 39 87
E design@eoos.com
www.eoos.com

Auftraggeber & Produzent
Client & Producer
Duravit AG
Werderstraße 36
D-78132 Hornberg
T +49 (0)7833 70-0
E info@duravit.de
www.duravit.de

Inipi B

Kompaktsauna . Compact sauna

Mit Abmessungen von gerade einmal 120 x 120 Zentimetern lässt sich dieses klassische Schwitzbad gut in die moderne Bad- und Wohnarchitektur integrieren, selbst in einer kleinen Stadtwohnung. Dank ihrer Versorgungsautarkie macht die Sauna auch Umzüge mit. Ziel war es, ein Produkt von höchstem Designanspruch für ein vergleichsweise geringes Budget zu entwickeln. Möglich wird dies durch die Konzentration auf das Wesentliche. Über ein integriertes Bedienfeld sind Temperatur, Timer und Uhr individuell einstellbar. Eine Eco-Funktion spart in Ruhephasen Energie. Vor dem nächsten Saunagang heizt der Ofen automatisch wieder auf. Die Kabine präsentiert sich puristisch und reduziert. Die großflächige Verglasung sorgt optisch für Transparenz.

With dimensions of only 120 by 120 centimetres, this classic sweat lodge easily integrates with residential and modern bathroom environments and can even be installed in small city apartments. Since it independently connects to supply units, it can also be taken along when its owner moves to a new place. The goal of developing a product of design excellence for comparably small budgets has been reached by concentrating on the most essential. An integrated control panel allows individual adjustment of temperature, timer, and clock, while an eco-mode ensures that energy is saved during stand-by phases. before the next sauna session, the heater will automatically bring the temperature to the desired level. The cabin has a puristic and reduced appearance, with the generous glazing ensuring transparency.

**Produktgestaltung | Industrial Design
Konsumgüter**
Design ausgewählt
**Product Design | Industrial Design
Consumer Goods**
Honourable Mention

Pandoretta

360° Wireless Audio System

Design
Thomas Feichtner
Schottenfeldgasse 55/1/6
A-1070 Wien
T +43 (0)676 966 38 65
E studio@thomasfeichtner.com
www.thomasfeichtner.com

Auftraggeber & Produzent
Client & Producer
Poet Audio GmbH
Sonnleitenweg 41
A-8043 Graz
T +43 (0)699 17 41 12 13
E markus.platzer@poetaudio.com
www.poetaudio.com

Dieses Rundum-Soundsystem empfängt dank seiner Ausstattung mit modernster Bluetooth-Technologie Musik kabellos über iPhone, Smartphone oder Computer. Sieben Lautsprecher und ein 170-Watt-Verstärker sorgen unabhängig von der Hörposition im Raum für eine Klangwiedergabe von höchster Qualität. In seiner Erscheinung und Materialität – verwendet werden Eichenholz und Edelstahl – erinnert »Pandoretta« eher an ein Musikinstrument als an ein Serienprodukt aus dem Bereich Consumer Electronics. Der Klangkörper ist beliebig platzierbar, die Töne können ungehindert in alle Richtungen ausstrahlen. Auf außen liegende Bedienelemente wurde konsequent verzichtet, da das System hauptsächlich über mobile Geräte angesteuert wird. Über zwei verborgene Schaltflächen kann es jedoch auch mechanisch bedient werden.

Thanks to its state-of-the-art bluetooth technology, this all-around sound system receives music wirelessly via iPhone, smartphone, or computer. Seven loudspeakers and a 170-watt amplifier ensure a sound performance of superior quality, regardless of the listener's position. With its appearance and materials used – oak and high-grade steel – »Pandoretta« is reminiscent of a musical instrument rather than a mass product from the consumer electronics industry. The sound box can be variably placed in a room, so that the sound is freely transmitted in all directions. The design consistently dispenses with control elements on the outside, since the system will usually work in combination with mobile devices. However, it can also be operated mechanically via two hidden control panels.

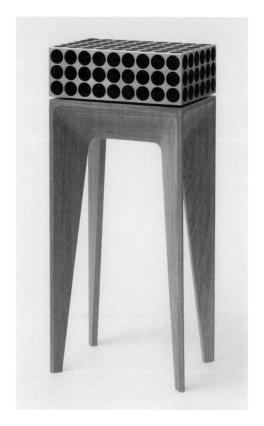

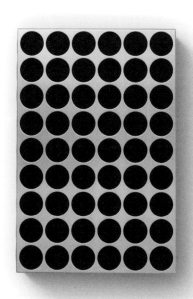

Produktgestaltung | Industrial Design
Konsumgüter
Design ausgewählt
Product Design | Industrial Design
Consumer Goods
Honourable Mention

Majestic – Woodstone Collection

Stein-Holz-Brillenfassung . Stone-and-wood spectacle frame

Design
ROLF Spectacles

Auftraggeber & Produzent
Client & Producer
ROLF – Roland Wolf GmbH
Mühlbachweg 6
A-6671 Weißenbach am Lech
T +43 (0)5678 20077
E office@rolf-spectacles.com
www.rolf-spectacles.com

Diese Brillenfassung geht nicht mit der Mode – die Konzentration liegt auf dem hochwertigen Material und seiner Verarbeitung. Zum Einsatz kommen hier ausschließlich natürliche Materialien wie Stein und Holz sowie neue, innovative Herstellungstechnologien. Feinster Endschliff in Handarbeit macht jedes Stück zu etwas ganz Besonderem, das man so schell nicht mehr ablegt. Dank der Holzscharniere enthält der Rahmen weder Metall noch Plastik und damit keine Allergene. Er ist extrem leicht, wartungsfrei und antistatisch. In der Form wurde das vorliegende Modell aus der Kollektion »Woodstone« von einem Oldtimer inspiriert: dem Daimler 104/Majestic.

This spectacle frame does not follow any fashion trends – its focus is on the superior quality of the material and how the latter is processed. Only such natural materials as stone and wood are employed to produce this item, as well as new, innovative manufacturing technologies. In the end, each piece is fine-tuned by hand, which makes it so unique that you will not want to take it off again. Featuring wooden hinges, the frame contains neither metal nor plastic and is therefore free of allergens. It is extremely light, maintenance-free, and anti-static. The shape of the present model from the »Woodstone« collection has been inspired by a vintage car: the Daimler 104/Majestic.

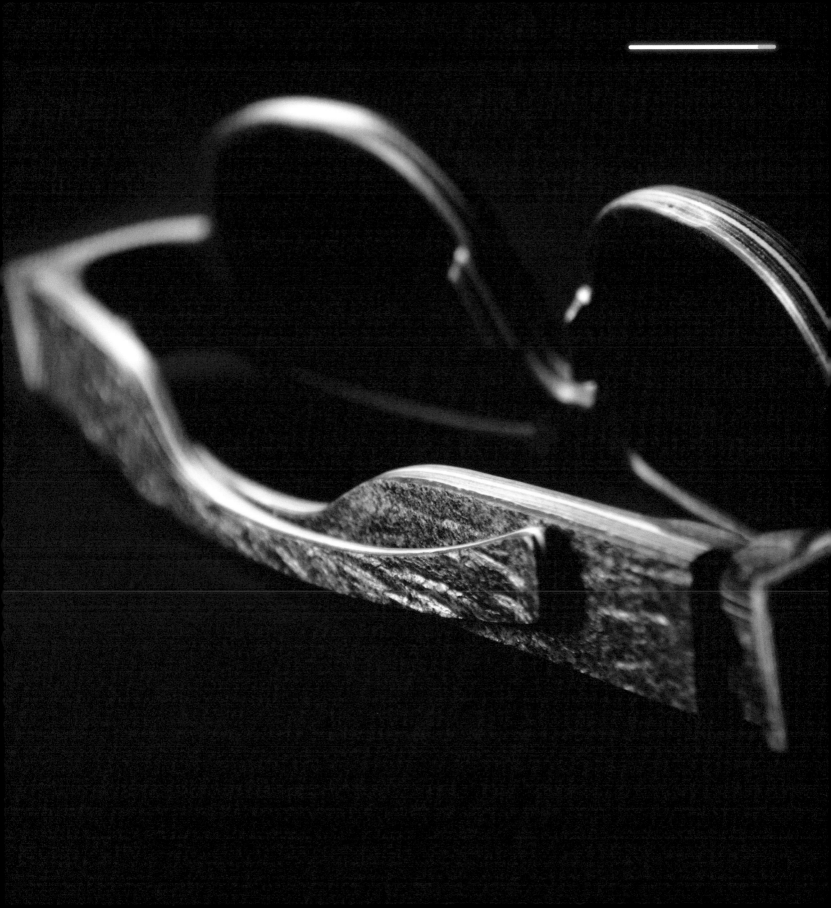

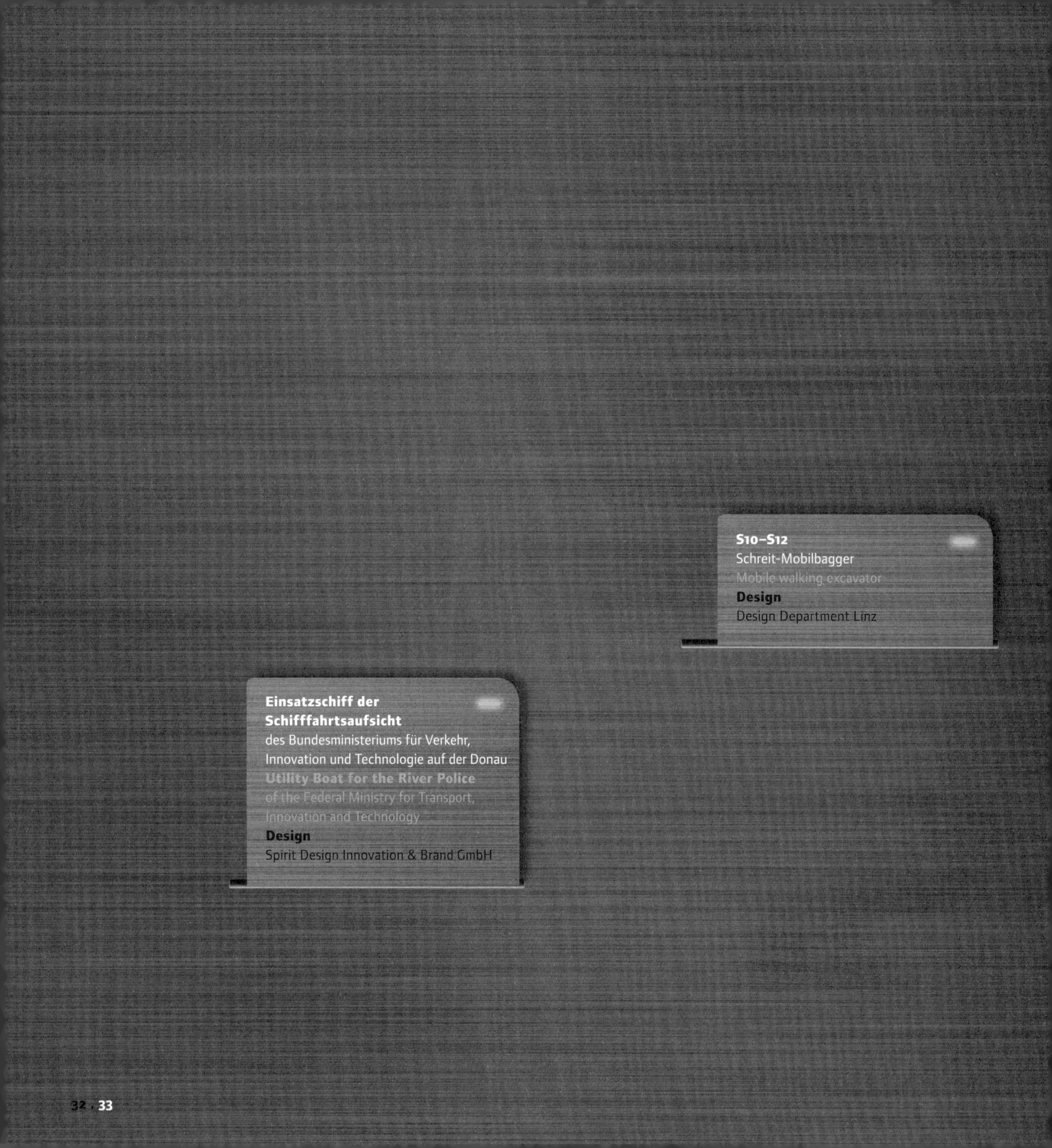

S10–S12
Schreit-Mobilbagger
Mobile walking excavator
Design
Design Department Linz

**Einsatzschiff der
Schifffahrtsaufsicht**
des Bundesministeriums für Verkehr,
Innovation und Technologie auf der Donau
Utility Boat for the River Police
of the Federal Ministry for Transport,
Innovation and Technology
Design
Spirit Design Innovation & Brand GmbH

Produktgestaltung
Product Design

Industrial Design
Industrial Design

Investitionsgüter
Capital Goods

Urban Sky
LED-Straßenleuchte
LED streetlight
Design
podpod design

Fronius AccuPocket
Schweißgerät
Welding machine
Design
formquadrat gmbh

Produktgestaltung | Industrial Design
Investitionsgüter
Staatspreis Design
Product Design | Industrial Design
Capital Goods
National Design Prize

Design
Spirit Design Innovation & Brand GmbH
Daniel Huber, Georg Bläsi,
Markus Tanzer-Kargl
Hasnerstraße 123
A-1160 Wien
T +43 (0)1 367 79 79-0
E spirit@spiritdesign.com
www.spiritdesign.com

Auftraggeber
Client
Bundesministerium für Verkehr,
Innovation und Technologie (bmvit)
Oberste Schifffahrtsbehörde
DI Reinhard Vorderwinkler
Radetzkystraße 2
A-1030 Wien
T +43 (0)1 711 62 65-0
E reinhard.vorderwinkler@bmvit.gv.at
www.bmvit.gv.at

Produzent
Producer
ÖSWAG Werft Linz AG Nfg. GmbH & Co KG
Hafenstraße 61
A-4010 Linz
T +43 (0)732 76 56-0
E office@oeswag.at
www.oeswag-werft.at

Einsatzschiff der Schifffahrtsaufsicht

des Bundesministeriums für Verkehr, Innovation und Technologie auf der Donau

Utility Boat for the River Police

of the Federal Ministry for Transport, Innovation and Technology

Dieses »Behördenschiff« dient als Arbeitsgerät zur Erfüllung eines breiten Aufgabenspektrums auf der internationalen Wasserstraße der Donau. Die fahrende Dienststelle übernimmt Verkehrsregelung und Notfallmanagement und stellt als Mischung aus Schnell-, Arbeits- und Transportboot eine ganz neue Schiffsklasse dar. In seiner Erscheinung vermittelt das Multifunktionsboot Zukunftsfähigkeit, Autorität und Sicherheit. Erreicht wird dies durch die sachliche, bewusst an die Stealth-Technologie angelehnte Formensprache und die schlichte Farbgebung in Weiß und Grau. Besonders geachtet wurde auch auf Wartungsfreundlichkeit und eine komfortable Arbeitsumgebung. Große Glasflächen bieten einen umfassenden Ausblick. Die Funktionen beinhalten neben Navigations- und Informationssystemen eine innovative Personenbergeeinrichtung, diverse Schleppmöglichkeiten, flexible Überstiegsstege und ein neues Feuerlöschsystem.

This »official« boat fulfils a wide spectrum of tasks on the international waterway of the Danube. A mixture of speedboat, transport boat, and workboat, this mobile duty station, which represents an entirely new type of watercraft, performs such functions as traffic regulation and emergency management. The appearance of this multifunctional boat suggests sustainability for the future, authority, and safety. This is achieved by an austere language of form that deliberately relies on stealth technology and the plain colour combination of white and grey. Particular attention has been paid to creating a convenient working environment and ensuring easy maintenance. Generous glass surfaces offer wide views. Besides navigation and information systems, the vessel is equipped with an innovative rescue device, various towing facilities, flexible gangways, and a new fire extinguishing system.

**Produktgestaltung | Industrial Design
Investitionsgüter**
Nominierung
**Product Design | Industrial Design
Capital Goods**
Nomination

S10–S12

Schreit-Mobilbagger . Mobile walking excavator

Design
Design Department Linz
Christian Kreiner, Stefan Oberhuemer
Landstraße 15/2. Stock
A-4020 Linz
T 43 (0)732 66 05 66
E c.kreiner@designdepartment.at
www.designdepartment.at

Auftraggeber & Produzent
Client & Producer
Kaiser AG Fahrzeugwerk
Vorarlbergerstrasse 220
FL-9486 Schaanwald
T +423 377 21 21
E kaiserag@kaiser.li, marketing@kaiser.li
www.kaiser.li

Die komplette Neugestaltung der S-Serie berücksichtigt optische Harmonie, komplexe Funktionen sowie einen stark verbesserten Fahrer- und Bedienkomfort und verbindet Dynamik mit Übersichtlichkeit. Dank einzeln teleskopierbarer Lafetten eignet sich der Bagger für Einsätze in extremen Schräglagen und im bis zu zwei Metern tiefen Wasser: Schwer zugängliches Gelände bei Hochwasser und nach Muren- und Lawinenabgängen ist für die Maschine kein Hindernis. Die Kabine und der asymmetrische Oberwagen bilden eine Einheit, die wiederum in einem ausgewogenen Verhältnis zum Unterwagen steht. Für optimale Standfestigkeit sorgt ein tiefer gelegter Schwerpunkt. Die Kabine bietet hervorragende Rundumsicht und eine komfortable Sitzposition. Im Inneren sorgen Grau- und Schwarztöne für ein ruhiges, konzentriertes Ambiente: Immerhin entspricht die Bedienung des Baggers in ihrer Komplexität der eines Helikopters. Im Außenbereich sorgen die Unternehmensfarben Blau und Gelb für Signalwirkung.

The complete redesign of the company's S-series combines dynamism and clarity and takes into account visual harmony, complex functions, and a strongly improved ride comfort and ease of use. Thanks to its individually telescopic legs, the excavator lends itself to operations on extremely steep slopes and in water to a depth of two metres: impassable terrain during floods and after landslides and avalanches is not an obstacle for this vehicle. Its cab and asymmetrical upper structure form a unit, which in turn is kept in perfect balance with the undercarriage. A lowered centre of gravity ensures maximum stability. The cabin offers a 360-degree view and a highly comfortable seat. Inside the cabin, grey and black provide for a calm, concentrated working ambience: after all, operating this excavator is as complex as steering a helicopter. The corporate colours of blue and yellow used for the vehicle's exterior have a signalling effect.

**Produktgestaltung | Industrial Design
Investitionsgüter**
Design ausgewählt
**Product Design | Industrial Design
Capital Goods**
Honourable Mention

Fronius AccuPocket

Schweißgerät . Welding machine

**Design
formquadrat gmbh**
Julian Pröll, Mario Zeppetzauer
Industriezeile 36
A-4020 Linz
T +43 (0)732 777 244
E office@formquadrat.com
www.formquadrat.com

**Auftraggeber & Produzent
Client & Producer
Fronius International GmbH**
Vorchdorfer Straße 40
A-4643 Pettenbach
T +43 (0)7242 241-0
E contact@fronius.com
www.fronius.com

Das akkubetriebene Elektrodenschweißgerät verbindet die beiden Unternehmensbereiche Schweißtechnik und Batterieladesysteme. Die Vorteile für den Benutzer sind Bewegungsfreiheit und Unabhängigkeit vom Stromnetz, sodass Arbeiten auch an schwer zugänglichen Orten durchgeführt werden können. Der Akku zeichnet sich durch geringes Gewicht und eine lange Lebensdauer aus. Mittels Schnellladefunktion ist das Gerät in etwa 30 Minuten wieder voll einsatzfähig. Die kantige Formensprache verleiht den Eindruck von Robustheit und Mobilität, während flächige Elemente für Ausgleich sorgen. Der ergonomisch geformte Kunststoffgriff reduziert das Gewicht und lädt mit seiner dynamischen Linienführung zum Greifen ein. Die dem Benutzer zugeneigte Bedienoberfläche garantiert gute Ablesbarkeit. Eingebettet in die Design-DNA des Unternehmens vereint die Gestaltung Ästhetik und Funktionalität.

This battery-operated electrode power welder unites the company's divisions of welding technology and battery charging systems. Benefits for users include being able to move freely and independently of an electric power supply when working in places difficult to access. The lightweight battery has a long life and, in fast-charge mode, can be recharged to be fully operable again within thirty minutes. The angular language of form, suggestive of robustness and mobility, is balanced by planar surfaces. The ergonomically shaped synthetic handle helps reduce weight and, thanks to its dynamically moulded outlines, invites a firm grip. The control panel is inclined towards the user to facilitate readability. Embedded in the company's design DNA, this product unites aesthetic qualities and functionality.

Produktgestaltung | Industrial Design
Investitionsgüter
Design ausgewählt
Product Design | Industrial Design
Capital Goods
Honourable Mention

Urban Sky

LED-Straßenleuchte . LED streetlight

Design
podpod design
Iris und Michael Podgorschek
Ferrogasse 10/4
A-1180 Wien
T +43 (0)1 479 12 12
E podpoddesign@mac.com
www.podpoddesign@com

Auftraggeber & Produzent
Client & Producer
Philips GmbH
Unternehmensbereich Lighting
Lübeckertordamm 5
D-20099 Hamburg
T +49 (0)40 2899-0
E gerd.wiesemann@philips.com,
office.austria@philips.com
www.philips.de,
www.ecat.lighting.philips.at

Die Form der Leuchte basiert auf einfachen Boole'schen Operationen mit geometrischen Grundkörpern. Mit ihrer Polarität zwischen rund und eckig ist sie überraschend komplex und ändert sich je nach Blickwinkel – sie öffnet oder schließt sich, lässt die Leuchte in den Hintergrund treten oder präsent sein. Die leicht angestellten Endflächen hellen die angrenzenden Hausfassaden dezent auf und machen die Leuchte auch im Straßenverlauf gut sichtbar. Der Holzmast mit seiner archaischen Anmutung tritt in einen reizvollen Kontrast zur LED-Technologie, die Einsparungen von bis zu 30 Prozent gegenüber konventionellen Leuchten ermöglicht. Gehäusegröße und -form sind auf eine optimale Wärmeableitung ausgelegt. Die Leuchte ist bei Reparatur und Entsorgung mit wenigen Handgriffen in ihre Bestandteile zerlegt.

The shape of this streetlight is based on simple Boolean operations with basic geometric bodies. Polarized between circular and angular, it is surprisingly complex and changes depending on the perspective – opening or closing, emphasizing the structure or obscuring it. Slightly slanted end faces direct the light upwards to discreetly illuminate the façades of buildings in the neighbourhood and ensure that the lamps are clearly visible along the course of a street. With its archaic appearance, the wooden pole creates a charming contrast to the modern LED technology employed here, which makes it possible to save up to 30 per cent of energy compared to common streetlights. The size and form of the cover were chosen with optimized heat conduction in mind. The lamp can easily be disassembled for repair or disposal.

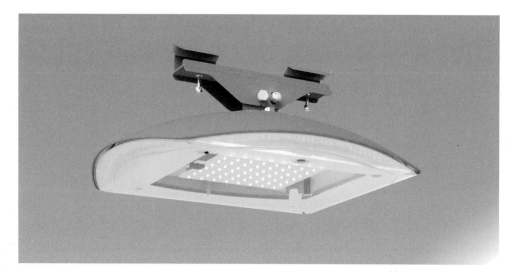
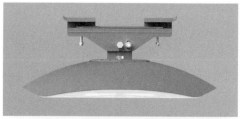
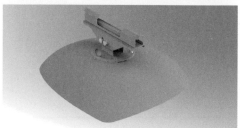

Perfekt Box
Hybridraum
Hybrid space
Design
Perfekt World & Kohlmayr Lutter Knapp

**Neuer Salzburger
Hauptbahnhof**
New Salzburg Central Station
Design
Kadawittfeldarchitektur GmbH

Every Body ...
Tiefgaragen-Installation
Underground parking installation
Design
White Elephant

**Ich lasse mich nicht länger
für einen Narren halten**
Ausstellungsgestaltung
**I won't let myself be fooled
any longer**
Exhibition design
Design
Celia Di Pauli & Eric Sidoroff

Amalienbad
Lichtdesign Schwimmhalle
Light design for an indoor swimming pool
Design
podpod design

Pixel im Turm
Das Hotel im Ennser Stadtturm
Pixels in the Tower
The hotel in the city tower of Enns
Design
Haas Architektur

Paradies der Blicke
Kultur-Themenweg in den Hochalpen
Panorama Paradise
Circuit trail in the High Alps
Design
Nofrontiere Design GmbH &
Xplan architecture

Räumliche Gestaltung
Staatspreis Design
Architectural Design
National Design Prize

Neuer Salzburger Hauptbahnhof
New Salzburg Central Station

Design
Kadawittfeldarchitektur GmbH
Aureliusstraße 3
D-52064 Aachen
T +49 (0)241 946 90-0
E office@kwa.ac
www.kadawittfeldarchitektur.de

Auftraggeber
Client
ÖBB Holding AG
Konzernkommunikation & Marketing
Clemens-Holzmeister-Straße 6
A-1100 Wien
T +43 (0)1 93000-44077
E kristin.hanusch-linser@oebb.at
www.oebb.at/holding

Umsetzung
Realization
ÖBB Infrastruktur AG
Projektleitung Nahverkehr Salzburg
Weiserstraße 7
A-5020 Salzburg
T +43 (0)662 93000-4065
www.oebb.at/infrastruktur

Der wichtigste Verkehrsknotenpunkt des Landes Salzburg wird seit 2008 bei laufendem Betrieb zu einem kombinierten Durchgangsbahnhof für den Nah- und Fernverkehr umgebaut. Hoher Kundenkomfort, kurze Wege, barrierefreies Umsteigen, eine zentrale Passage mit Einkaufsmöglichkeiten und die Integration denkmalgeschützter Bauteile in eine hochmoderne Bahninfrastruktur geben der Festspielstadt ein unverwechselbares Entree. Hier wird eindrucksvoll gezeigt, dass eine Verknüpfung von historischer Substanz (1860–1909) mit moderner Architektur auch bei Großprojekten des öffentlichen Verkehrs möglich ist. Die alte Stahlhalle wurde in die neue Bahnsteigüberdachung integriert. Die dynamischen Bahnsteigdächer bilden mit den filigranen historischen Bahnsteighallen eine überraschende Einheit. Auch der Hausbahnsteig mit seinen 40 Gusseisensäulen wurde in die neuen Bauten einbezogen. Die quer zu den Bahnsteigen geführte und nach oben offene Passage unterhalb der Gleise gibt den Blick bis unter die historische Stahlhalle frei. Der neue Bahnhof wird mit einer eigenen Erdwärmeanlage geheizt und gekühlt.

With work beginning in 2008, the most important transit hub in the state of Salzburg has been transformed while in full operation into a combined through station for suburban and intercity railway transportation. A high level of customer convenience, short distances, barrier-free train transfers, a central shopping arcade, and the integration of cultural heritage into a state-of-the-art railway infrastructure provide the festival city with a unique entree. The solution impressively demonstrates that a fusion between historical building substance (1860–1909) and modern architecture is also possible in large-scale public transport projects. The old steel concourse has been incorporated into the new platform roofing, whose dynamic appearance forms a surprising union with the filigree historical platform halls. The main platform, with its 40 cast iron columns, has been imbedded in the new structures. The arcade, running transverse to the platforms and underneath the tracks, is open at the top and offers a view of the historical steel concourse. The new railway station is heated and cooled by its own geothermal energy plant.

Räumliche Gestaltung
Nominierung
Architectural Design
Nomination

Perfekt Box

Hybridraum . Hybrid space

Design
Perfekt World
Matzingerstraße 21/1–4
A-1140 Wien
T +43 (0)650 999 35 59
E mail@perfektworld.net
www.perfektworld.net

Kohlmayr Lutter Knapp
Büro für systemisches Design
Favoritenstraße 17
A-1040 Wien
T +43 (0)650 773 9 773
E office@klk.ac
www.klk.ac

Auftraggeber & Produzent
Client & Producer
Perfekt World

Den Kern des Hybridraums bildet eine Aluminiumbox in den Ausmaßen von 1,70 x 6 x 2,50 Metern, die sich im oberen Teil des Raumes befindet und 70 unterschiedlich dimensionierte Rahmen beinhaltet. Es ergibt sich ein flexibler Ausstellungs- Präsentations-, Lager- und Arbeitsraum, der sich immer neu an die jeweiligen Inhalte anpasst. Die Box bietet optimale Raumnutzung und auf den Zweck abgestimmte Lösungen, ist aber auch selbst ein wandelbares Kunstwerk. Eine Perfekt Box befindet sich im Wiener MuseumsQuartier, quartier 21, Electric Avenue.

The core of this hybrid space consists of an aluminium box measuring 1.70 by 6 by 2.50 metres that is installed in the upper section of a room and contains as many as 70 differently dimensioned frames. The system provides a flexible space for exhibitions, presentations, storage, and work that can always be adapted to the respective contents and needs. The box therefore offers solutions tailor-made to suit momentary purposes, and an optimal use of space. On the other hand, it is a work of art in itself. A Perfekt Box is installed at the Vienna MuseumsQuartier, quartier 21, Electric Avenue.

Every Body …

Tiefgaragen-Installation . Underground parking installation

Design
White Elephant
Florian Puschmann, Tobias Kestel
Klosterwiesgasse 14
A-8010 Graz
T +43 (0)650 39 39 427
E florian.puschmann@white-elephant.at
www.white-elephant.at

Kurator
Curator
Georg Dinstl

Auftraggeber
Client
Weitzer Hotels BetriebsgmbH
Grieskai 12
A-8020 Graz
T +43 (0)316 703-0
E hotel@weitzer.com
www.weitzer.com

Ausführung
Realization
Florian Duderstadt & Martin Huth
August-Musger-Gasse 20
A-8010 Graz
T +43 (0)699 109 20 390, (0)699 135 54 696
E office@betont.at
www.betont.at

Die Installation befindet sich an einem zentralen Punkt in einer Tiefgarage, den alle Autofahrer beim Hinein- oder Hinausfahren passieren. Sie besteht aus einem 30 Meter langen Raster aus 700 lackierten Aluminiumlamellen, die einem zweiten Raster aus Plakatpapier vorgelagert sind. Durch die Bewegung des Betrachters und die Veränderung des Blickwinkels ergibt sich ein Moiré-Effekt, der dynamische Schlieren erzeugt und einen eingebetteten Text lesbar macht. Ein an und für sich trister Ort erfährt durch die Installation, die sich mit Wahrnehmung während eines Bewegungsvorgangs auseinandersetzt, eine Aufwertung.

This installation is located at a central point in an underground car park that is passed by all drivers when entering or exiting. It consists of a 30-metre-long screen composed of 700 coated aluminium lamellas and mounted in front of a second screen covered with poster paper. The movement of the beholder and the resulting change in perspective produce a moiré effect of dynamic streaks through which an embedded text becomes readable. Thanks to the installation, which deals with perception while the beholder is in motion, a normally dreary place is enhanced.

Räumliche Gestaltung
Design ausgewählt
Architectural Design
Honourable Mention

Design
Celia Di Pauli & Eric Sidoroff
Mariahilfpark 3
A-6020 Innsbruck
T +43 (0)699 19 09 24 37
E office@sid-architekten.at
www.sid-architekten.at

Kuratorin
Curator
Lisa Noggler

Auftraggeber
Client
Interreg IV-Projekt Psychiatrische
Landschaften

Südtiroler Landesarchiv /
Geschichte und Region
Armando-Diaz-Straße 8
I-39100 Bozen
T +39 (0)471 411 940
E siglinde.clementi@provinz.bz.it
www.provinz.bz.it/landesarchiv/

Universität Innsbruck
Institut für Geschichtswissenschaften und
europäische Ethnologie
Institut für Erziehungswissenschaften
Innrain 52
A-6020 Innsbruck
T +43 (0)512 507-0
E maria.heidegger@uibk.ac.at
www.psychiatrische-landschaften.net

Ausführung
Realization
Deko Trend
Badenerstraße 27
A-2514 Traiskirchen
T +43 (0)2252 508 330
E office@dekotrend.at
www.dekotrend.at

Ich lasse mich nicht länger für einen Narren halten

Ausstellungsgestaltung

I won't let myself be fooled any longer

Exhibition design

Diese Wanderausstellung erzählt das Schicksal von 30 Frauen und Männern, die zwischen den 1830er- und 1970er-Jahren im Raum Tirol psychiatrisch behandelt wurden. Sorgfältig recherchierte Fallgeschichten in Buchform sind in den einzelnen Stationen der Schau nachzulesen. Die flexible, transportable, zerlegbare und zugleich robuste Szenografie lässt sich in ganz unterschiedliche Räume integrieren, behauptet sich dabei jedoch selbst als »Raum im Raum«. Die Gestaltung arbeitet mit Codes – Möbelstücken, Gegenständen, Situationen –, die allgemeinen Vorstellungsklischees entsprechen, sowie mit der Farbe Weiß. Die Besucher werden so dazu angeregt, die Rolle der Patienten einzunehmen. Minimal »falsch« – etwas zu eng, hoch oder gerade – proportionierte Ausstellungsmöbel machen die beklemmenden Lebensumstände auch körperlich spürbar.

This travelling exhibition relates the fates of thirty women and men undergoing psychiatric treatment in the region of Tyrol between the 1830s and 1970s. Carefully researched case histories in the form of books can be consulted at the individual stations of the show. The flexible, transportable, yet robust scenography can easily be disassembled and integrates with various types of locations while at the same time asserting itself as a »room within a room«. The design is based on codes – pieces of furniture, objects, situations – corresponding to common stereotypes, as well as on the colour white. Visitors are encouraged to adopt the roles of patients. Exhibition furniture dimensioned slightly out of proportion – a bit too narrow, high, or straight – makes the oppressive circumstances in which these people lived perceptible, also physically.

Pixel im Turm
Das Hotel im Ennser Stadtturm

Pixels in the Tower
The hotel in the city tower of Enns

Design
Haas Architektur
Linzer Straße 18a
A-4470 Enns
T +43 (0)7223 8 11 56
E office@haasarchitektur.at
www.haasarchitektur.at

Auftraggeber
Client
Stammtisch der Herren zu Ens
c/o Oellinger Enns Steyr GmbH & Co KG
Dr.-Renner-Straße 19
A-4470 Enns
T +43 (0)7223 82 181-888
E vorstand@herrenzuens.org
herrenzuens.org, www.turmhotel.at

Ausführung
Realization
Arge Restauratoren – reiterjohann@aon.at
Kurt Reiss – restaurator.reiss@aon.at
Expert Leitner, Elektro Leitner GmbH –
office@expert-leitner.at
Franz Leitner GmbH – www.franz-leitner.at
LH Holzbau GmbH – www.lh-holzbau.at
Seyrlehner GmbH – www.seyrlehner.at
Tischlerei Anzinger e. U. – www.anzinger.at
Bodingbauer Glas GmbH –
www.glas-bodingbauer.at
Stadtgemeinde Enns, Bauhof der Stadt Enns –
www.enns.at
Haas Architektur – www.haasarchitektur.at

Das Pixel-Hotel besteht aus Zimmern, die sich nicht in einem einzelnen Gebäude befinden, sondern sich über eine ganze Stadt oder einen Landstrich verteilen. Hier wurde in der ehemaligen Türmerwohnung des Ennser Stadtturms aus dem 16. Jahrhundert ein Hotelzimmer eingerichtet. Das »Pixelzimmer« in 20 Metern Höhe bietet einen einzigartigen Ausblick. Bei der Renovierung wurde der Raum mit modernem Komfort ausgestattet. Den ursprünglichen Lattenboden hat man freigelegt und restauriert. Der Sanitärbereich wurde neu gestaltet: Eine Lichtkuppel im Gewölbe gibt den Blick auf die alte Bausubstanz frei; satinierte Glaswände machen den Raum in seiner Gesamtheit spürbar. Das zentral platzierte quadratische Bett kann in jeder Richtung benutzt werden, wodurch sich immer wieder neue Blickbeziehungen ergeben. Das Projekt zeichnet sich durch einen sensiblen Umgang mit der Historie und deren gelungene Verbindung mit zeitgemäßer Gestaltung aus.

The Pixel Hotel consists of rooms that are not located in a single building, but scattered across an entire city or region. Here a hotel room has been installed in the chamber formerly occupied by the watchman of the city tower of Enns, which dates from the sixteenth century. The so-called »Pixel Room«, located at a height of 20 metres, offers a unique view. During the renovation the room was furnished with modern conveniences, while the original plank floor was exposed and restored. The sanitary area presents itself in a completely new design: through a skylight in the vault, one can catch a glimpse of the old building substance, satin glass walls ensure that the room is perceived in its entirety. The square bed, placed at the centre, can be used in any direction, so that ever-new perspectives open up. This project is characterized by a sensitive approach to history and its satisfactory fusion with contemporary design.

Amalienbad

Lichtdesign Schwimmhalle . Light design for an indoor swimming pool

Design
podpod design
Iris und Michael Podgorschek
Ferrogasse 10/4
A-1180 Wien
T +43 (0)1 479 12 12
E podpoddesign@mac.com
www.podpoddesign@com

Auftraggeber
Client
Magistratsabteilung 44 – Bäder
Reumannplatz 23
A-1100 Wien
T +43 (0)1 60 112-0
E kunden@ma44.wien.gv.at
www.wien.gv.at/freizeit/baeder/

Ausführung
Realization
Art for Art – www.artforart.at
Elektro Leonbacher – www.leonbacher.at

Die aus den 1970er-Jahren stammenden Leuchten des Wiener Jugendstilbads, erbaut 1923–1926 nach dem Vorbild einer römischen Therme, wurden gegen neue Beleuchtungskörper ausgetauscht, die möglichst unauffällig integriert wurden und dabei die historische Architektur betonen. Linearstrahler unter den Balkonen erhellen die Zone um das Becken. In den Gängen dahinter liefern LED-Leuchten Direktlicht; eine stimmungsvolle Aufhellung der Decken akzentuiert diese in Türkis, Goldgelb oder Weiß. Der Beckenbereich wird vom Dachumgang aus beleuchtet. Die tonnenförmige Hallendecke wird von den oberen Säulen aus mit LED-Strahlern aufgehellt. Damit bei Dunkelheit die Glasoberlichten nicht als schwarze Löcher erscheinen, wird mittels LED-Strahlern ein zartblauer Mondscheineffekt simuliert. Farbsteuerbaren LED-Leisten verwandeln den Sprungturm in eine effektvolle Bühne. Vorprogrammierten Lichtszenarien, abzurufen über Touch Screen, sorgen für die richtige Stimmung beim Schwimmunterricht, Wellness-Programm oder Turmspringen. Trotz der Erhöhung des Lichtniveaus konnte der Energieverbrauch um 57% reduziert werden.

The old lighting from the 1970s of this public indoor swimming pool in Vienna, built in 1923–26 in the style of Art Nouveau and based on Roman baths, has been replaced by new lights. They have been integrated into the historical architecture as unobtrusively as possible, emphasizing it at the same time. Linear spots mounted underneath the galleries illuminate the area around the pool. In the passageways behind, LED lights supply direct light, while the ceilings may be accentuated in turquoise, golden yellow, or white. The pool itself is lit from the roof gallery. The barrel vault ceiling of the main hall is highlighted with LEDs from the upper columns. In order to prevent the skylights from appearing as black holes at night, a pale blue moonlight effect may be simulated with LED spots. Colour-changing LED bars transform the diving platform into a dramatic stage. Pre-programmed light scenarios, retrievable via touch screen, deliver the appropriate atmosphere for swimming instruction, wellness, or diving. Although the light level has been increased, it has been possible to reduce energy consumption by 57 per cent.

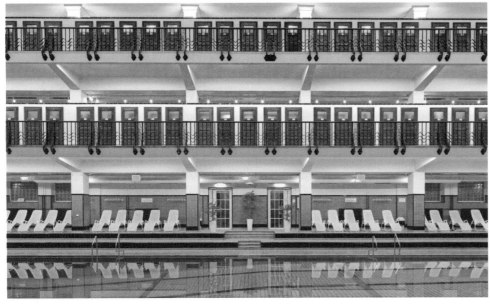

Räumliche Gestaltung
Design ausgewählt
Architectural Design
Honourable Mention

Paradies der Blicke
Kultur-Themenweg in den Hochalpen
Panorama Paradise
Circuit trail in the High Alps

Design
Nofrontiere Design GmbH &
Xplan architecture
Alexander Szadeczky, Wolfgang Windbüchler,
Alexander Egger, Manfred Hlina
Belvederegasse 26
A-1040 Wien
T +43 (0)1 985 57 50
E ask@nofrontiere.com
www. nofrontiere.com

Auftraggeber
Client
Niederösterreichische
Schneebergbahn GmbH
Bahnhofplatz 1
A-2734 Puchberg am Schneeberg
T +43 (0)2742 36 099 099
E office@schneebergbahn.at
www.schneebergbahn.at

Ausführung
Realization
Nofrontiere Design GmbH

Hier wurde für den Schneeberg, ein Tourismus-
gebiet mit Tradition, eine multimediale Gesamt-
inszenierung entwickelt, die in mehreren Stationen
Geschichte und kulturelle Bedeutung zeitgemäß
vermittelt und zugleich herrliche Ausblicke bietet.
Die Lösung besticht durch Infotainment und
architektonische Kommunikation. Ein weitläufiger
Ausstellungs- und Veranstaltungssaal befindet
sich in der einstigen Bergstation der Zahnrad-
bahn. Gegenpole wie Natur und Kultur oder reale
und virtuelle Welt ergeben ein spannungsreiches
Zusammenspiel. Die Formensprache erstreckt sich
konsistent über Architektur, Leitsystem, Outdoor
Möbel und grafische Elemente.

This multimedia circuit trail has been developed for
the Schneeberg, a traditional tourist region in the
Alpine foothills. Consisting of several stations, it
conveys information about the area's history and
cultural significance while offering breathtaking
views. The solution stands out for its infotainment
value and architectural communication. A generous
exhibition and performance hall has been installed
in the old mountain station of the cog railway.
Such antipodes as nature and culture and the
real and virtual worlds merge to make an exciting
combination. The language of form consistently
runs through the architectural elements, wayfin-
ding system, outdoor furniture, and graphic design
elements.

EDU Buch
Integration neuer Medien in den Schulalltag
EDU Book
Integration of new media into day-to-day
school life
Design
Helene Steiner

EDU Spind
Kommunikationssystem für Schulen
EDU Locker
Communication system for schools
Design
Helene Steiner

Fred/Fold
Klappbike
Folding bike
Design
toka OG

Sporty Supahero
High-Tech-Radfahrerjacke
High-tech cycling jacket
Design
Utope

Treehugger
3-in-1-Forstmaschine
3-in-1 forestry machine
Design
AberJung OG

EDU Spind

Kommunikationssystem für Schulen

EDU Locker

Communication system for schools

Design
Helene Steiner
Franzensgasse 13/12
A-1050 Wien
E info@helenesteiner.com
www.helenesteiner.com

Das Projekt bietet eine kostengünstige und rasch umsetzbare Lösung, die zur Individualisierung des Schulalltags und zu einer optimalen Nutzung der Einrichtung Schule beiträgt. Bedürfnisse und Wünsche von Schülern und Lehrenden wurden in einer Feldstudie erhoben und berücksichtigt. Jeder Schüler/jede Schülerin verfügt über einen persönlichen Spind, der als Postfach, Stauraum und Ladestation für elektronische Geräte dient. Dadurch sollen die Kommunikation gefördert, interne Abläufe optimiert und die Integration neuer Medien in den Unterricht verbessert werden.

This project offers an inexpensive and swiftly realizable solution that contributes to the individualization of day-to-day school life and an optimal utilization of the school as an institution. The needs and desires of students and teachers were collected in a field study and taken into consideration in the development of the concept. Each student has his or her personal locker, which serves as a mailbox, storage, and charging station for electronic devices. This is to promote communication, optimize processes, and improve the integration of new media into tuition.

Design
Helene Steiner
Franzensgasse 13/12
A-1050 Wien
E info@helenesteiner.com
www.helenesteiner.com

EDU Buch
Integration neuer Medien in den Schulalltag

EDU Book
Integration of new media into day-to-day school life

Die Integration neuer Medien und die Optimierung von Kommunikation in der Schule sind die zentralen Aufgaben dieses Projekts, das eine Brücke zwischen analoger und digitaler Welt bildet. Das Handy wird zum Schulcomputer. Legt man es auf das EDU Buch, schaltet es sich automatisch in den Schulmodus ohne Telefonier- und SMS-Funktion, öffnet die auf den Schulalltag abgestimmte Software und erweckt das robuste, flexible, leichte und kostengünstige EDU Buch zu digitalem Leben. Es ersetzt nicht nur Taschenrechner, Overheadprojektor und PC, sondern bietet sich auch für Recherchen außerhalb des Schulgebäudes an. Analoge Arbeiten können mit der Kamera dokumentiert und digital verarbeitet werden. Zukunftsvision: Das EDU Buch bringt Bildung in Entwicklungsländer – es verbraucht kaum Strom, kann nicht veralten, weil sich die Software mit dem Handy updatet, und ermöglicht freies Lernen in Kombination mit dem Internet.

The integration of new media and the optimization of communication at school are the central tasks of this project, which builds a bridge between the analogue and digital worlds. The mobile phone transforms into a school computer. When placed on EDU Book, it automatically switches to school mode, without telephone and SMS functions. It opens the software adapted to the needs of school life and brings the robust, flexible, lightweight, and inexpensive EDU Book to digital life. It not only replaces pocket calculator, overhead projector, and PC, but also lends itself to doing research outside the school building. Analogue works can by documented with the camera and processed digitally. A vision of the future: EDU Book takes education to developing countries. Its electricity consumption is extremely low; it cannot become obsolete because the software is updated via the mobile phone; and in combination with the Internet, it facilitates free learning.

HAUSAUFGABE FÜR MONTAG :
BUCH ~~SAMSUNG~~ SEITE 11 – BIOLOGIE
AUFGABE 2 – BIS FREITAG

Fred/Fold

Klappbike . Folding bike

Design
toka OG
Tobias Bernstein
Kurzegasse 4
A-6850 Dornbirn
T +43 (0)5572 89 02 45
E office@toka-design.com
www.toka-design.com

Der Fokus bei der Gestaltung dieses klappbaren Bikes für den urbanen Raum liegt auf einem dynamischen und schlichten Erscheinungsbild. Der Klappmechanismus ist visuell unauffällig gehalten, um die klare Geometrie der Rahmendreiecke nicht zu stören. Die einseitigen Achsen der Laufräder unterstützen die optische Einfachheit; gleichzeitig wird durch die Asymmetrie eine gewisse Spannung aufgebaut. Das Gelenk des Klappmechanismus besteht aus zwei in den Monocoque-Rahmen einlaminierten Hohlzylindern, in denen eine Achse eingelagert ist. Per Inbus kann der Schließmechanismus gelöst und der Rahmen geklappt werden.

The focus in the design of this folding bike, which is destined for use in urban environments, has been on its dynamic and unpretentious appearance. The folding mechanism has been kept inconspicuous so as not to disturb the clear geometry of the triangles formed by the frame. The overall visual simplicity is enhanced by the one-sided axles of the bicycle wheels; simultaneously, a certain amount of visual tension is created by the resulting asymmetry. The joint of the folding mechanism consists of two hollow cylinders laminated into the monocoque frame and accommodating a pivot. The locking mechanism can be released by an Allen wrench, allowing the frame to be folded.

Treehugger

3-in-1-Forstmaschine . 3-in-1 forestry machine

Design
AberJung OG
Elisabethstraße 88/2/6
A-8010 Graz
T +43 (0)660 17 000 44
E office@aberjung.com
www.aberjung.com

Diese ästhetisch ansprechende Maschine vereint die Vorteile eines Harvesters mit jenen eines Forwarders. Zudem ist sie extrem steigfähig und zugleich straßentauglich. Verschiedene Modi ermöglichen ein breites Einsatzgebiet, von herkömmlichen Durchforstungsarbeiten bis hin zur Aufarbeitung nach Sturmschäden. Das hybride Antriebssystem ist dank niedriger Schadstoffemissionen und leisem Elektrobetrieb besonders umweltschonend. Darüber hinaus sorgen das geringe Gewicht und ein innovatives Reifenkonzept für Bodenschonung. Die Gestaltung der Fahrerkabine bietet optimale Sicht und Sicherheit. Sowohl formal als auch funktional bezieht der »Treehugger« seine Inspiration aus der Insektenwelt.

This aesthetically appealing machine combines the merits of a harvester with those of a forwarder. Moreover, it can climb extreme slopes, while it can also easily be driven on ordinary roads. Various modes ensure a wide spectrum of applications, from common thinning to clear-up work after storm damage. The hybrid engine is extremely easy on the environment, thanks to a low level of polluting emissions and a low-noise electric drive. In addition, the vehicle's reduced weight and innovative tyre system protect the forest ground. The design of the driver's cab offers optimal visibility and safety. Both formally and functionally, »Treehugger« draws its inspirations from the world of insects.

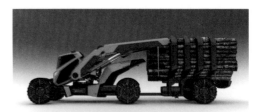

DesignConcepts
Auszeichnung
Honourable Mention

Sporty Supahero

High-Tech-Radfahrerjacke . High-tech cycling jacket

Design
Utope
Wolfgang Langeder
Wiesengang 5
A-4209 Engerwitzdorf
T +43 (0)699 125 785 42
E utope@utope.eu
www.utope.eu

Mitarbeit
Collaboration
Fraunhofer-Institut für Zuverlässigkeit
und Mikrointegration (IZM)
Gustav-Meyer-Allee 25
D-13355 Berlin
T +49 (0)30 46 403-0
www.izm.fraunhofer.de

In die High-Tech-Jacke für urbane Nomaden ist ein mikroelektronisches System integriert, das LEDs, Sensoren, Steuerungselemente, einen Schalter sowie eine aufladbare Batterie umfasst. Diese Teile sind so verkapselt, dass sie sicher in der Benutzung und waschbar sind. Eine der Hauptfunktionen besteht darin, den Träger bei Dunkelheit sichtbar zu machen. Weitere Entwicklungen sollen Diebstahlschutz, die Messung von Körper- und Umgebungsdaten und eine Navigation durch die Stadt ermöglichen. Die intelligenten Materialen sind dehnbar und zugleich robust und sorgen für Schutz vor Wind und Wetter. Modedesign und Technologie verschmelzen hier zu einem sinnvollen Ganzen, sodass die Jacke dem digitalen Lebensstil von heute gerecht wird.

A microelectronic system comprising LEDs, sensors, control elements, a switch, and a rechargeable battery is embedded in this high-tech jacket for urban nomads. All of these parts are insulated in such a way that they can safely be used and washed. One of the garment's principal functions is to make the cyclist visible in the dark. Further developments are meant to provide anti-theft protection, measurements of physical and environmental data, and navigation through a city. The jacket's intelligent materials are both elastic and robust and protect the wearer in wind and adverse weather. Here fashion design and technology merge to form a sensible whole, so that the jacket does justice to today's digital lifestyle.

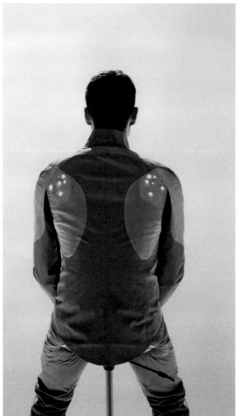

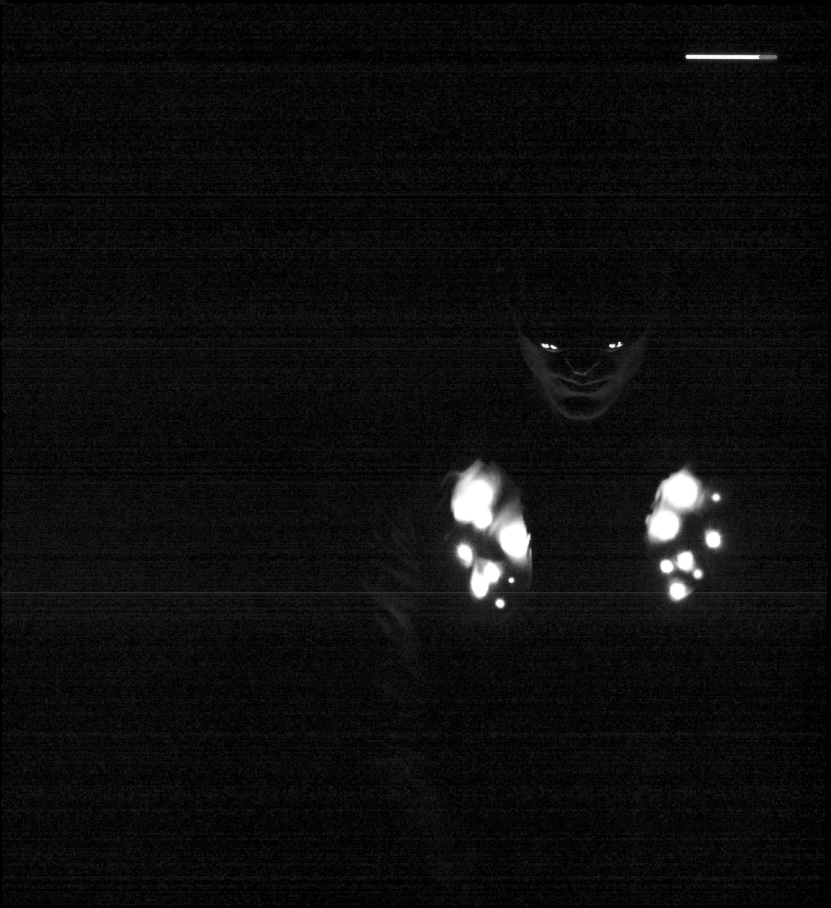

Fritz Frenkler

Günther Grall

Stefanie Grüssl

Gerald Kiska

Karin Polzhofer

Sabine Pümpel

Johann Scheuringer

Mitglieder der Jury
Jury Members

Fritz Frenkler

Diplomdesigner, CEO f/p design deutschland gmbh und f/p design japan inc.,
Ordinarius für Industrial Design, Technische Universität München (TUM)

www.f-p-design.com, www.id.ar.tum.de

Statement

Für künftige Jurys wäre es sehr zu empfehlen, mit physischen Produkten zu arbeiten, soweit deren Abmessungen dies erlauben. Auf diese Weise wären wichtige Designaspekte wie Ergonomie, Materialgerechtigkeit und Funktionalität besser nachvollziehbar. Nur in bestimmten Fällen – etwa bei Übergröße oder im Bereich der räumlichen Gestaltung – sollten Fotodokumentationen oder gar Computerzeichnungen zugelassen werden. Zudem wäre es wünschenswert, weitere österreichische Unternehmen und Designer für die Teilnahme an diesem Wettbewerb zu gewinnen. Ich weiß, dass es noch viel mehr gute Produkte in Österreich gibt, die ich bei der Jurierung leider nicht gesehen habe. Dem Veranstalter gebührt herzlicher Dank für die Einladung zur Teilnahme an der Jury zum Staatspreis Design 2013 in Wien.

Kurzbiografie

Fritz Frenkler studierte Industrial Design an der Hochschule für Bildende Künste in Braunschweig. Er war lange Zeit Geschäftsführer von frogdesign Asien in Tokio und der wiege Wilkhahn Entwicklungsgesellschaft sowie Design-Chef der Deutschen Bahn AG. Im Jahr 2000 gründete er mit Anette Ponholzer die f/p design deutschland gmbh und 2003 f/p design japan inc. Fritz Frenkler ist Regional Advisor des International Council of Societies of Industrial Design (ICSID), Montreal. Seit vielen Jahren ist er Vorstandsmitglied des iF Industrie Forum Design, Hannover, und seit 1997 Juryvorsitzender des iF product design award. Zudem ist er Gründungsmitglied des universal design e.V., Hannover, und seit 2013 Mitglied der Akademie der Künste in Berlin. 2005 wurde er zum Honorarprofessor im Studiengang Industrial Design an der Hochschule für Bildende Künste Braunschweig ernannt. Seit 2006 ist Fritz Frenkler Universitätsprofessor (Ordinarius) für Industrial Design der Fakultät für Architektur an der Technischen Universität München.

f/p design gmbh: Stapelstuhl »Amos 870« für Kokuyo
f/p design gmbh: stacking chair »Amos 870« for Kokuyo

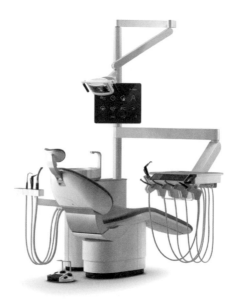

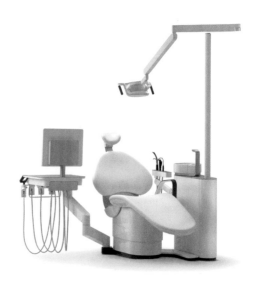

f/p design gmbh: dentale Behandlungseinheit »Soaric« für Morita
f/p design gmbh: dental chair unit »Soaric« for Morita

Designer, CEO f/p design deutschland gmbh and f/p design japan inc.,
Full University Professor of Industrial Design, Munich University of Technology (TUM)

www.f-p-design.com, www.id.ar.tum.de

Statement

For future jury sessions I would highly recommend working with real products as far as their dimensions permit. In this way it would be easier to judge such important design aspects as ergonomics, material appropriateness, and functionality. Only in certain cases – when a product is too large, or for architectural design solutions – should photo documentations or computer renderings be admitted. It would also be desirable to persuade more Austrian companies and designers to participate in this contest. I do know that there are many more excellent products in Austria that were unfortunately not entered. My warmest thanks are due to the organizer for inviting me to take part in the jury for the National Design Prize 2013 in Vienna.

Short Biography

Fritz Frenkler studied industrial design at the Academy of Fine Arts (HBK) in Braunschweig. Over an extensive period of time, he was managing director of frogdesign Asia in Tokyo, managed the company wiege Wilkhahn Entwicklungsgesellschaft, and worked as head designer for the German railway company, Deutsche Bahn AG. In 2000 he founded f/p design germany gmbh with Anette Ponholzer, followed by f/p design japan inc. in 2003. Fritz Frenkler is a regional advisor to the International Council of Societies of Industrial Design (ICSID), Montreal. For many years he has been a board member of iF Industrie Forum Design, Hanover, and since 1997 has been jury chairman of the iF product design award. Moreover, he is a founding member of universal design e. V., Hanover, and since 2013 has been a member of the Berlin Academy of Fine Arts. In 2005 he was appointed honorary professor at HBK Braunschweig. Since 2006, Fritz Frenkler has been university professor holding the chair for Industrial Design in the Department of Architecture at the Munich University of Technology (TUM).

Studienarbeiten,
Lehrstuhl für Industrial Design, TUM
Student works,
Chair for Industrial Design, TUM

Modulares Flugzeugkabinenkonzept »Modulair«
Modular aircraft cabin concept »Modulair«
Design
Marvin Bratke, Daniel Jakovetic, Sandro Pfoh, Daniel Tudman
Betreuung . Supervision
Fritz Frenkler, Wotan Wilden

Wandkühlschrank »Widefrigde«
Wall-mounted fridge »Widefrigde«
Design
Fabian Bosch, Fabian Arun Ghosal, Jan König,
Felix Koppmann, Evelyn Pinter
Betreuung . Supervision
Fritz Frenkler, Matthias Hajek

Unterdruck-Aufbewahrungssystem »Frischhalten«
Vacuum storage system »Frischhalten«
Design
Tilman Bona, Clemens Kössler, Matthias
Leyendecker, Maximilian Reiner, Laura Ann Walter
Betreuung . Supervision
Fritz Frenkler, Matthias Hajek

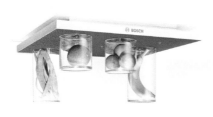

Günther Grall

Diplomdesigner, Leiter und Professor des Studiengangs
Design und Produktmanagement, FH Salzburg

www.fh-salzburg.ac.at

Statement

Wie wir wissen, ist Design ist ein wichtiger Motor
unserer Wirtschaft. Design ist Innovationstreiber
und kann strategisch genutzt werden, um das Neue
in Produktentwicklungen gezielt zu kommunizie-
ren. In Anbetracht der Bandbreite und Qualität
der für den Staatspreis eingereichten Projekte und
auch in Kenntnis einiger hervorragender – leider
nicht eingereichter – Arbeiten ist mir um unsere
Wirtschaft nicht bange. Dieses kleine Österreich ist
wahrlich ein Designland. Die Tage in dieser hoch-
karätigen Jury waren anstrengend, aber interessant
und lehrreich. Ich danke für die Möglichkeit, dass
ich dabei sein konnte. Verbesserungsvorschläge?
Warum sollte die Jury nicht auch ein über die eingereichten Arbeiten hinausgehendes Vorschlags-
recht haben? Und: Vielleicht wäre ein zweistufiges
Verfahren mit Serienmodellen in der letzte Runde
dazu angetan, die Entscheidung mit ruhigerem Gewissen zu treffen. Letztlich hätten in jeder Sparte
einige der nominierten Produkte den Staatspreis
verdient.

Kurzbiografie

Nach der HTL für Tischlerei & Raumgestaltung
war Günther Grall als Trendscout und Planer für
Restaurants, Bars und Discotheken tätig. Ein ge-
stalterisch herausforderndes Tischler-Meisterstück
ebnete ihm den Weg an die Kunstuniversität Linz.
Nach Abschluss des Diplomstudiums Industrial Design bei Professor Horst Meru und Praxisjahren bei
Kiska Creative Industries folgte ein Auslandsstudi-
um am Art Center College of Design in Pasadena,
Kalifornien. Nach der Rückkehr arbeitete Günther
Grall fünf Jahre bei Bene Büromöbel im Design und
Produktmanagement und zeichnete unter anderem
für die speziell für die Erste Bank entwickelten
Möbel im Kassen- und Selbstbedienungsbereich
verantwortlich. Dann holte ihn Meru als Assistent
zurück an seine Meisterklasse. Neben der wissen-
schaftlichen Arbeit an der Dissertation über Form-
strukturphasen war dies für ihn auch eine produk-
tive Zeit als selbständiger Designer für Firmen wie
Fischer, Banner Batterien oder Rosensteiner. 2002
folgte der Ruf nach Salzburg, um dort den Studiengang Design und Produktmanagement aufzubauen,
der auf die Bedürfnisse von KMU zugeschnitten
ist und markenspezifisches Design im Fokus hat.
Heute leitet Günther Grall neben Bachelor- und
Masterstudiengang auch die Forschungsgruppe
DE RE SA (Design Research Salzburg), die sich mit
der Objektivierung von Entscheidungskriterien im
Produktentwicklungsprozess für Auftraggeber wie
Adidas, BMW oder Trilety beschäftigt.

Batterie »Uni Bull« für Banner Batterien
Battery »Uni Bull« for Banner Batterien

Designer, Professor and Head of the Design and Product Management Course of Studies, Salzburg University of Applied Sciences

www.fh-salzburg.ac.at

Statement

As we all know, design is an important motor in our economy, as well as a driver of innovation that can be strategically employed in order to communicate novelties in product development in a target-oriented way. Recognizing the broad spectrum and the quality of the works competing for the National Design Prize and aware of the fact that there are even more excellent projects that have unfortunately not been submitted, I am not in the least worried about the Austrian economy. This small country is truly a design nation. Serving on this high-calibre jury was challenging, but also interesting and enlightening; I am grateful for having been granted the opportunity to participate. My suggestions for improvement? Why should the jury not also have the right to recommend products apart from those entered? And perhaps a two-tier process, with serial models in the final round, would contribute to making decisions with a clearer conscience. After all, in each of the categories there were several products that would have deserved to win the National Design Prize.

Short Biography

Having graduated from a higher technical secondary school for cabinetmaking and interior design, Günther Grall worked as a trend scout and planner for restaurants, bars, and music clubs. An ambitious masterpiece as a cabinetmaker paved his way to the Linz University of Art and Design. After completing his studies in industrial design under Professor Horst Meru and several years of practical work with Kiska Creative Industries, Günther Grall went abroad to study at the Art Center College of Design in Pasadena, California. Upon his return to Austria, he began working in design and product management for the office furniture manufacturer Bene, where among the projects he was responsible for was the furniture specially developed for the service and self-service zones of Erste Bank. After five years Meru called him back to his master class at the university as his assistant. While working on his doctoral dissertation on the phases of formal structuring, he also experienced a productive period as a freelance designer in the service of such companies as Fischer, Banner Batterien, and Rosensteiner. In 2002 he was appointed to the faculty of the Salzburg University of Applied Sciences, where he helped set up the study course for Design and Product Management, tailored to the needs of SMEs and with a focus on brand-specific design. Besides directing the bachelor's and master's courses offered by his school, today Günther Grall also heads the research group DE RE SA (Design Research Salzburg), which is involved in objectifying criteria for decision-making in the product development process for such clients as Adidas, BMW, and Trilety.

Klauenpflegestand »Top 5« für Rosensteiner
Hoof trimming crush »Top 5« for Rosensteiner

Stefanie Grüssl

Designerin und Mitarbeiterin des Bundesministeriums
für Wirtschaft, Familie und Jugend

www.bmwfj.gv.at

Statement

Hervorragendes Design unterstreicht die Alleinstel-
lungsmerkmale eines Produkts, kommuniziert die
Unternehmensphilosophie und ist daher erfolgs-
entscheidend. In diesem Sinn wurden auch heuer
wieder viele spannende Projekte ausgezeichnet.
Auffallend beim Staatspreis Design 2013 war, dass
vermehrt Stühle und medizinisch-technische Produkte in neuen Formen und Varianten produziert
und eingereicht wurden. In der Kategorie der
räumlichen Gestaltung gab es einige Überraschun-
gen; der Staatspreisträger überzeugt durch eine
gesamtheitliche Lösung hinsichtlich der Kombination historischer und moderner Bauweise.

Kurzbiografie

Stefanie Grüssl absolvierte eine handwerklich-
künstlerische Ausbildung in der Abteilung
Keramik und Ofenbau an der Ortweinschule in
Graz (Leitung Prof. Anna Losert) und studierte
Produktgestaltung bei Professor Matteo Thun-
Hohenstein an der Universität für angewandte
Kunst in Wien. Nach ihrer Mitarbeit bei Designer-
legende Leslie L. Lane in Klagenfurt gründete sie
ihr eigenes Designbüro, dessen Schwerpunkte auf
den Bereichen Produktentwicklung, Messestand-
bau, Ausstellungsgestaltung, Katalogproduktion,
CI-Entwicklung und Erstellung von Storyboards für
die Filmwirtschaft lagen. Nach dem Ortswechsel
nach Wien ist Stefanie Grüssl seit 1999 Mitarbeiterin des Wirtschaftsministeriums und dort zuständig
für Designfragen und die Abwicklung der vom
Wirtschaftsministerium ausgelobten Staatspreise.
Von 2000 bis 2004 war sie Vorstandsmitglied der
Österreichischen Designstiftung. Neben ihrer admi-
nistrativen Tätigkeit widmet sie sich der Fotografie
und Malerei und unterstützt dabei soziale Themen
wie die Vinzi-Rast-Projekte von Cecily Corti.

Coverfoto und Fotobeiträge für den Jubiläumsband
»100 Jahre Regierungsgebäude – Ein Haus und seine Geschichte«
von Verena Hahn-Oberthaler und Gerhard Obermüller
Cover photograph und photography for the anniversary
publication »100 Years Government Building – A House and Its
History« by Verena Hahn-Oberthaler and Gerhard Obermüller

Designer and Member of the Staff of the Ministry
of Economy, Family and Youth

www.bmwfj.gv.at

Statement

Outstanding design enhances the unique selling
propositions of a product, conveys the philosophy
of a company, and is therefore decisive for its success. Along these lines, numerous exciting projects
have once again been selected in this year's design
award scheme. What made itself particularly felt
at the 2013 National Design Prize is the increasing
number of chairs and medical engineering solutions
that are currently being produced in new variants
and shapes. The architectural design category held
several surprises. Here the winner of the National
Design Prize convinced the jury with a holistic concept combining historical and modern architecture.

Short Biography

Stefanie Grüssl received an artistic and industrial
education in th Department of Ceramics and
Tile Stove Construction at the Ortwein Higher
Secondary School for Art and Design in Graz (under
Prof. Anna Losert) and studied product design with
Prof. Matteo Thun-Hohenstein at the University of
Applied Arts in Vienna. After working with designer
legend Leslie L. Lane in Klagenfurt, she opened her
own design office, which focused on product
development, trade fair architecture, exhibition
design, catalogue production, CI development,
and storyboards for the film industry. Following
her move to Vienna, Stefanie Grüssl joined the
Federal Ministry of Economy in 1999, where she is
responsible for design matters and the adminis-
tration of the various award schemes offered by
the Federal Ministry of Economy. Between 2000
and 2004 she was a board member of the Austrian
Design Foundation. Apart from her administrative
duties, she devotes herself to photography and
painting and supports such social initiatives as the
Vinzi Rast projects for the homeless, organized by
Cecily Corti.

Konzept und Fotografie für den Jubiläumskalender
»100 Jahre Regierungsgebäude Stubenring 1913–2013«
Concept and photography for the anniversary calendar
»100 Years Government Building Stubenring 1913–2013«

Foto Kalenderblatt Dezember
Photograph for the month of December

Gerald Kiska

Diplomdesigner, CEO KISKA GmbH

www.kiska.com

Statement

Der Staatspreis Design hat bezogen auf die Einreichungen, das Format und die Produktpräsentation ein ungeheures Potenzial. Allerdings war die Bewertung nicht immer einfach, speziell, weil das reale Produkt nicht vorlag. Die Einreichungen in diesem Jahr lassen auf mehr davon hoffen – und es gibt wesentlich »mehr davon« in Österreich!

Kurzbiografie

Gerald Kiska absolvierte die Hochschule für künstlerische und industrielle Gestaltung in Linz und arbeitete anschließend in verschiedenen Designbüros und Agenturen im In- und Ausland, darunter 1984/85 bei Interform Design in Wolfsburg, 1985/86 bei Form Orange in Hard, 1986 bei Idea in Stuttgart und schließlich bei Porsche Design in Zell am See. 1991 gründete er sein eigenes Designunternehmen in Anif bei Salzburg, das heute nicht nur flächenmäßig (5.000 Quadratmeter), sondern auch hinsichtlich der Mitarbeiterzahl (über 120 Mitarbeiter aus 20 Nationen) eines der größten eigentümergeführten Studios Europas ist. Bekannt wurde Gerald Kiska durch seine Arbeiten für den Motorradhersteller KTM, für den er nicht nur die Hausfarbe Orange kreierte, sondern als Design- und Entwicklungsleiter sämtliche KTM-Fahrzeuge und Kommunikationsmaterialien verantwortet. 1994/95 lehrte er als Gastprofessor an der Hochschule für Gestaltung Offenbach am Main, von 1995 bis 2002 engagierte er sich als Mitbegründer und Dozent des Studiengangs Industrial Design an der Fachhochschule Joanneum in Graz und bis 2003 hatte er eine Gastprofessur an der Universität für Gestaltung Linz inne. Gerald Kiska arbeitet für ein breites Spektrum an Branchen, darunter Automobil, Konsumgüter, Nahrungsmittel & Getränke, Investitionsgüter und professionelle Werkzeuge. Der Schwerpunkt liegt auf der Entwicklung und Stärkung von Marken.

Zielfernrohr »Victory HT« für Zeiss
Rifle scope »Victory HT« for Zeiss

Fernglas »Victory HT« für Zeiss
Binoculars »Victory HT« for Zeiss

Pelletofen »Topo« für RIKA . Pellet stove »Topo« for RIKA

Kästle-Produktsortiment . Kästle product range

Straßenleuchte »Streetlight 10« für Siteco
Road lighting »Streetlight 10« for Siteco

Designer, CEO KISKA GmbH

www.kiska.com

Statement

In terms of entries, format, and product presentation, the National Design Award has a huge potential. However, judging proved to be not always so easy, especially because the real products were not present. This year's submissions hold the promise of more of the same – and there is certainly »more of it« in Austria!

Short Biography

Gerald Kiska graduated from the University of Art and Design in Linz and subsequently worked for various design offices and agencies in Austria and abroad, including Interform Design in Wolfsburg in 1984/85, Form Orange in Hard in 1985/86, Idea in Stuttgart in 1986, and finally Porsche Design in Zell am See. In 1991 he founded his own design office in Anif near Salzburg, which today is one of the largest owner-managed design studios in Europe, not only in terms of floor space (5,000 square metres), but also regarding the number of employees (more than 120 from twenty nations). Gerald Kiska became known for his work for the motorbike manufacturer KTM. Not only did he create the company's corporate colour of orange, but as head of design and development he is also responsible for the entire range of KTM's vehicles and the company's visual communication. In 1994/95 Gerald Kiska was a guest professor at the University of Art and Design in Offenbach am Main; between 1995 and 2002 he was involved with the Joanneum University of Applied Sciences in Graz as a co-founder of and lecturer in the industrial design course; and until 2003 he held the position of visiting professor at the University of Art and Design in Linz. Gerald Kiska works for a wide spectrum of industries, including automobile, consumer goods, food & beverage, capital goods, and professional tools. The focus of his activity is on developing and strengthening brands.

Sportwagen »X-Bow« und Motorrad »Super Duke« für KTM
Sports car »X-Bow« and motorbike »Super Duke« for KTM

Strahler »Comet« für Planlicht . Spotlight »Comet« for Planlicht

Elektro-Zweisitzer »RAKe« für Opel
Electric two-seater »RAKe« for Opel

Karin Polzhofer

Marketingleiterin KAPO Holding GmbH/Neue Wiener Werkstätte

www.kapo.co.at, www.neuewienerwerkstaette.com

Statement

Um Österreichs Position als Designland zu festigen, kann es meiner Ansicht nach nicht genug Initiativen und Leistungsschauen im Designbereich geben. Der Staatspreis Design ist ein wichtiges Signal im In- und im Ausland. Es gilt, die vielen herausragenden Arbeiten und das Potenzial unserer Designer und Unternehmen zu präsentieren und damit das kollektive Selbstbewusstsein zu stärken und nach außen zu tragen. In unserem Familienunternehmen arbeiten wir in der Produktentwicklung seit Jahrzehnten eng mit Kreativen zusammen. Um diese Zusammenarbeit zu intensivieren, haben wir im letzten Jahr selbst einen neuen Preis für Interieur-Design ins Leben gerufen, den NWW Design Award. Unser Ziel ist die Verbindung von traditionellem Handwerk mit hochwertigem Design, um Produkte zu schaffen, die emotionalisieren. Wichtig ist dabei, dass Produzent und Designer sich auf Augenhöhe treffen und Leidenschaft für das gemeinsame Werk einbringen. Die Vielfalt der Einreichungen beim heurigen Staatspreis Design zeigt, wie viele unterschiedliche Bereiche Design durchdringt und wie interdisziplinär Designer arbeiten müssen. Design ist dabei heute oft das entscheidende Kriterium, um sich mit seinem Produkt zu differenzieren. Design erzeugt Mehrwert und ist die Basis für Erfolg. Als Jurymitglied habe ich mich über die zahlreichen Einreichungen und den spannenden Diskurs mit den anderen Juroren gefreut und hoffe auch in Zukunft auf leidenschaftliches »Design made in Austria«.

Kurzbiografie

Nach ihrem Studium der Publizistik- und Kommunikationswissenschaften und Kunstgeschichte an der Universität Wien war Karin Polzhofer im ORF-Marketing als Produktmanagerin für das Kulturprogramm tätig. Mit der Übergabe des Familienunternehmens an Karin Polzhofer und ihre beiden Brüder übernahm sie die Leitung des Bereichs Marketing und verantwortet seit 2008 die Vermarktung von KAPO Fenstern und Türen und der Neuen Wiener Werkstätte. Der Familienbetrieb in vierter Generation ist seit 1927 auf die Herstellung hochwertiger Produkte aus Holz spezialisiert und beschäftigt heute rund 250 Mitarbeiter am Produktionsstandort Pöllau in der Südoststeiermark. Mit einem berufsbegleitenden MBA an der Executive Academy der Wirtschaftsuniversität Wien fundierte Karin Polzhofer ihre Erfahrungen im Bereich Marketing und Sales. Karin Polzhofer wurde 2009 mit dem EUF Award für erfolgreiche Nachfolge-Unternehmerinnen ausgezeichnet; 2010 erhielt sie den Living Culture Lady Award und 2011 war sie Zweitplatzierte beim Prix Veuve-Clicquot für die Unternehmerin des Jahres. 2013 wurde das Unternehmen für die Initiative des NWW Design Award für den Staatspreis Marketing nominiert.

Neue Wiener Werkstätte »Modern«
Neue Wiener Werkstätte »Modern«

Neue Wiener Werkstätte »Klassik«
Neue Wiener Werkstätte »Classics«

Marketing Director, KAPO Holding GmbH/Neue Wiener Werkstätte

www.kapo.co.at, www.neuewienerwerkstaette.com

Statement

As I see it, there cannot be enough initiatives and design awards, all of which contribute to firmly establishing Austria's position as a design country. The National Design Prize is an important signal both at home and abroad. In order to build a collective self-confidence and render it visible, it is necessary to present the outstanding achievements and potentials of the country's designers and companies. In our family enterprise we have been closely cooperating with creatives for decades in the development of our products. For the sake of intensifying this collaboration, we have launched a new prize for interior design, the NWW Design Award. Our goal is to combine traditional crafts-manship and high-quality design in the creation of products that appeal to the emotions. In such an endeavour it is essential for manufacturer and designer to communicate on a par with each other and passionately devote themselves to their joint project. The great diversity of entries submitted for this year's National Design Prize illustrates how de-sign has permeated many different fields and that designers need to work in a highly interdisciplinary fashion. Today design is frequently a vital criterion for a company to set itself apart with its product. Design creates added value and is the foundation for success. As a member of the jury, I was thrilled to see such a large number of submissions and discuss them with my colleagues. I hope that we will continue to see passionate »Design Made in Austria« in the future.

Short Biography

After her studies in journalism, communication science, and art history at the University of Vienna, Karin Polzhofer worked in the marketing depart-ment of the Austrian Broadcasting Corporation ORF as a product manager for the network's cultural programme. When she and her two broth-ers took over the family business, she was put in charge of the company's marketing and since 2008 has been responsible for the commercialization of KAPO windows and doors und the furniture of the Neue Wiener Werkstätte. The family enterprise, which is meanwhile run by the fourth generation, has specialized in the production of high-quality products made from wood since 1927. With its production site located in Pöllau in southeastern Styria, it currently has some 250 employees. While working for her own company, Karin Polzhofer completed an MBA programme at the Executive Academy of Vienna's University of Economics and Business in order to theoretically underpin her experience in marketing and sales. In 2009, Karin Polzhofer received the EUF Award honouring top female successors of commercial enterprises; in 2010 she received the Living Culture Lady Award and in 2011 came in second at the Prix Veuve-Clicquot for the Business Woman of the Year. In 2013 the company was nominated for the National Marketing Prize for its launch of the NWW Design Award.

KAPO Fenster und Türen . KAPO windows and doors

KAPO Fenster und Türen . KAPO windows and doors

Sabine Pümpel

Programmleitung »impulse«, Austria Wirtschaftsservice GmbH (aws)

(in beratender Funktion, ohne Stimmrecht) | www.impulse-awsg.at

Statement

Der Sonderpreis DesignConcepts wurde von »impulse« I aws mit dem Ziel initiiert, eine Brücke zum Staatspreis Design zu schlagen, der herausragende Produkte auszeichnet, die am Ende ihrer Entwicklung im Markt angekommen sind. DesignConcepts dagegen würdigt kreative Leistungen, die erst am Beginn ihres Entwicklungsweges stehen. Ihnen kann eine »impulse« I aws-Förderung helfen, Staatspreisträger von morgen zu sein.

Unter den 166 Einreichungen zum Staatspreis Design 2013 haben sich 34 für den Sonderpreis DesignConcepts beworben. Die im Rahmen dieses Awards vergebenen Preise kommen drei Projekten zugute: allen voran dem Kommunikationssystem »EDU Spind«, das für den schulischen Alltag eine modulare, flexible und kostengünstige Lösung anbietet. Die Schule ist auch im Fokus von »EDU Buch«, einem auf Smartphones einsetzbaren Tool für analoges und digitales Lernen. Gleichfalls ausgezeichnet wurde von der Jury das leichtgewichtige Klappbike »Fred/Fold« aus Karbon, das sich mit einem einfachen Handgriff auf 40 Prozent seines Volumens reduzieren und in jedem Kofferraum verstauen lässt. Wir freuen uns, dass auch heuer unter den Einreichungen und Nominierungen wieder Designprojekte sind, die in ihrer Entwicklungsphase bereits von »impulse« I aws unterstützt wurden.

Qualität und Diversität der Einreichungen sind ein vitales Spiegelbild des Kreativwirtschaftsstandortes Österreich. Junge Designerinnen und Designer können Wirtschaft und Industrie sowie Handel wie Gewerbe neue, unverbrauchte und unkonventionelle Ideen anbieten, die mit ihrer Nutzenstiftung kommende Bedürfnisse vorwegnehmen. Nicht zu übersehen sind bedeutende innovative Impulse für unsere Gesellschaft und ihren Lebensraum, welche die Akteure der Kreativwirtschaft in Stadt und Land setzen – von Gesundheit bis Urban Gardening, im Social Design wie im Bereich der neuen Medien. Kreativität und Innovationsfähigkeit sind

die Asse im globalen Wettbewerb. Das bestätigt »impulse« I aws darin, diese entscheidenden Wettbewerbsfaktoren zu fördern.

Kurzbiografie

Seit 2004 entwickelt und verstärkt Sabine Pümpel effiziente Impulse für die österreichische Kreativwirtschaft – bis 2006 als Programmleiterin der Arge »ImpulsProgramm creativwirtschaft«, ab 2007 innerhalb der Austria Wirtschaftsservice GmbH (aws). Der Fokus ihres Kompetenzbereichs liegt auf der Konzeption und inhaltlichen Weiterentwicklung der direkten monetären Fördermaßnahmen sowie auf den begleitenden Aktivitäten in den Bereichen Weiterbildung und Awareness innerhalb der heimischen Creative Industries. 2010 war die Expertin der Kreativwirtschaft mitverantwortlich für die Etablierung von FISA, der Initiative des Wirtschaftsministeriums zur Filmförderung. Die gebürtige Vorarlbergerin studierte nach einjährigem Aufenthalt in Berkeley, USA, Handelswissenschaften an der Wirtschaftsuniversität Wien und war danach u. a. im Produktmanagement der Konzerne Kraft Foods/Milka sowie IKEA tätig.

Projektbooklets . Project booklets

Biogasbetriebenes Arbeits- und
Transportfahrzeug »Ox«
Biogas-operated utility and transport
vehicle »Ox«
Spirit Design Innovation and Brand GmbH,
www.spiritdesign.com

Management of »impulse« Funding Programme, Austria Wirtschaftsservice GmbH (aws)

(in an advisory role, without vote) | www.impulse-awsg.at

Statement

The DesignConcepts Award was initiated by »impulse« I aws with the goal in mind of building a bridge to the National Design Prize, which highlights products that have finally arrived on the market, their development complete. The DesignConcepts scheme, on the other hand, honours creative efforts that are still at the very beginning of their evolution. These may be helped by funding through »impulse« I aws in order to become National Design Prize winners of tomorrow.

Of the 166 submissions entered in the contest for the National Design Prize 2013, as many as 34 applied for the DesignConcepts Award. Three projects will benefit from prizes distributed within our award scheme: first of all, the »EDU Locker« communication system, which provides for a modular, flexible, and inexpensive solution for everyday school life. School education is also in the focus of »EDU Book«, a tool for analogue and digital learning applicable in combination with smartphones. Finally, the jury also selected the lightweight folding bike »Fred/Fold«, which is made of carbon fibre and can easily be reduced to 40 per cent of its volume, so that it will fit into any car trunk. We are happy to note that this year, too, there are design projects among the submitted and nominated projects that were supported by »impulse« I aws during their development stages.

The quality and diversity of this year's entries vividly reflect Austria as a country of the creative industries. Young designers can offer our economy, industry, commerce, and trade new, fresh, and unconventional ideas that due to their value-in-use anticipate the needs to come. The vital innovative impulses delivered to our society and its urban and rural environments by the players in the creative industries cannot be overlooked; they range from health care and urban gardening to social design and new media. Creativity and the capacity for in-novation are assets in global competition. This confirms »impulse« I aws in its efforts to strengthen these essential competitive factors.

Short Biography

Sabine Pümpel has devised and enhanced efficient incentives for the creative industries in Austria since 2004 – until 2006 as head of the work group »ImpulsProgramm creativwirtschaft« and from 2007 on within the Austria Wirtschaftsservice GmbH (aws). Her competencies revolve around the conception and further evolution of direct funding measures, as well as such concomitant activities as advanced training and promoting awareness within the domestic creative industries. In 2010 she was also jointly responsible for the establishment of FISA, a film promotion initiative launched by the Federal Ministry of Economy, Family and Youth. Born in Vorarlberg, Sabine Pümpel spent one year in Berkeley, California, and then studied international business at the Vienna University of Economics and Business. She subsequently worked in product management for such international corporations as Kraft Foods/Milka and IKEA.

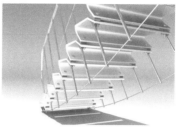

Innovatives Treppensystem »lufttritt 3.0«
nach dem Prinzip Hängebrücke
Innovative staircase »lufttritt 3.0«,
based on the principle of suspension bridges
Thomas Schiefer, www.lufttritt.at

Unrunder Ball »Corpus« zur Förderung von Reaktion, Koordination und Konzentration
Non-circular ball »Corpus« for training response, co-ordination, and concentration
Rasenreich, Mario Sinnhofer e. U., www.rasenreich.com

Johann Scheuringer

Geschäftsführender Gesellschafter Josko Fenster und Türen GmbH

www.josko.at

Statement

»Ganz schön schön« war es für mich, in dieser sympathischen Jury mitzuwirken. Für mich ist Design ein ganz natürlicher und wichtiger Bestandteil eines Produktes, Gebäudes oder Kommunikationsmittels. Es gibt kein Nicht-Design – es gibt nur gutes oder weniger gutes Design bzw. gute oder weniger gute Architektur. Ich bevorzuge die angloamerikanische Bedeutung des Begriffs Design als Gesamtlösung inklusive Konzept und Technik, die über den »kreativen«, gestalterischen Aspekt, der im deutschsprachigen Raum im Vordergrund steht, hinausgeht. Gerade ältere Produkte wie zum Beispiel Oldtimer (Geländewagen, Rennwagen), Möbel oder Elektrogeräte (Braun) zeigen uns auf einzigartige Weise, wie rein funktionales Design am nachhaltigsten, aber auch am schönsten sein kann. Heute würde man von Reduktion sprechen, damals war es oft natürliche, technische Notwendigkeit. Da heute so viele Produkte und Mitbewerber am Markt sind, läuft Design immer wieder Gefahr, zu viel zu wollen und seine Selbstverständlichkeit und seinen Mehrnutzen dabei zu verlieren. Am meisten beindrucken mich neue Konzepte, die durch ihre andere Sicht bzw. Neukonfiguration der Dinge ein völlig neuartiges Erlebnis bringen. Naturgemäß geht damit auch ein »anderes« Design einher. Dann ist auch der für mich wichtigste Aspekt, nämlich der des verbesserten Nutzens (nicht nur in ästhetischer Hinsicht) für den User, gegeben. Das versuchen wir auch bei Josko zu leben. Fenster und Türen »funktionieren« für sich allein ja nicht. Nur im Gebäude eingebunden können sie dem Gesamtkonzept nutzen oder im schlimmsten Fall auch schaden. Auf jeden Fall sollten sie sich integrieren – funktional und optisch. Ich sage seit Jahren scherzhaft: »Wir arbeiten erfolgreich daran, unsere Produkte im Haus verschwinden zu lassen.« Produkte wie unser rahmenloses Ganzglassystem »FixFrame« oder unsere wandintegrierten MET-Innentüren schaffen das sehr kompromisslos.

Kurzbiografie

In der Holzfachschule Hallstatt gab es erste Berührungspunkte mit dem Thema Möbel und Architektur. Nach einem längeren USA-Aufenthalt folgte ein Communications-Design-Studium am Art Center College of Design Europe. 1995 stieg Johann Scheuringer in das elterliche Fenster- und Türenunternehmen ein. Es wurde begonnen, Josko als nationale Marke aufzubauen und verstärkt durch ein eigenständiges Design der Produkte zu positionieren. Seit 2000 ist Johann Scheuringer Geschäftsführer für die Bereiche Marketing und Entwicklung. Und seit 2006 definiert sich das Unternehmen klar als design- bzw. architekturorientiert. Diese Ausrichtung drückt sich im Slogan »Ganz schön schön. Ganz schön Josko« aus. Josko wurde mehrmals mit dem oberösterreichischen Wirtschaftspreis Pegasus sowie als bestes Familienunternehmen Oberösterreichs (Austria's Leading Companies) ausgezeichnet. Darüber hinaus kann das Unternehmen eine dreifache Auszeichnung beim red dot award: product design und Nominierungen sowohl zum deutschen als auch zum österreichischen Staatspreis Design vorweisen.

Fenster »Safir« . Window »Safir«

Managing Partner, Josko Fenster und Türen GmbH

www.ktm-bikes.at

Statement

It was »quite simply« a valuable experience for me to participate in this congenial jury. For me, design is a natural and essential part of a product, building, or means of communication. Non-design does not exist – there is only good or less good design and good or less good architecture. I prefer the Anglo-American interpretation of the term, according to which design is a holistic solution that includes the concept and engineering parts and therefore goes beyond the »creative« aspect, which is key in the German-speaking area. Especially older products, such as vintage cars (cross-country vehicles, racing cars), furniture, or electrical appliances (Braun), impressively demonstrate that purely functional design is most sustainable, but can also be exceptionally beautiful. What we would now call reduction was frequently a normal technological necessity. As today's market is flooded with products and competitors, design often runs the risk of wanting to achieve too much, thereby forfeiting its simplicity and additional benefits. What impresses me most are innovative concepts offering an entirely new experience through an unusual perspective or a reconfiguration of things. Naturally, this always goes hand in hand with a »different« design. Only then will the criterion that seems most important to me, namely that of a – not merely aesthetically – greater benefit for the user, be met. This is what we aspire to achieve at Josko. Windows and doors do not »function« by themselves. Only when embedded in a building can they be of advantage – or, in the worst case, of disadvantage – to an overall concept. In any case, they should integrate, both functionally and visually. I always say as a joke: »We successfully work to make our products disappear in the house.« This is uncompromisingly accomplished with such products as our frameless full-glass system »FixFrame« or our wall-integrated MET interior doors.

Short Biography

Johann Scheuringer first came in touch with furniture and architecture at the Hallstatt Woodworking School. Following an extensive stay in the USA, he studied communications design at the Art Center College of Design Europe. In 1995 he entered the family business, a company producing windows and doors, beginning to build and strengthen Josko as a national brand and position it on the market with the aid of distinctive product design. Since 2000, Johann Scheuringer has been a managing partner in charge of marketing and development. And since 2006, the company has unmistakably defined itself as design- and architecture-oriented. This orientation is also expressed in the company's slogan »Quite simply beautiful. Quite simply Josko«. Josko has repeatedly been awarded the Pegasus Prize for Upper Austrian industries and has been honoured as Upper Austria's best family-owned enterprise (Austria's Leading Companies). Moreover, the company has won three red dot awards: product design and has been nominated for both the German and Austrian National Design Prize.

Fenster »Topas« . Window »Topas«

Haustür »Nevos«, Lärche natur . Front door »Nevos«, natural larch

Von der »guten Form« zum »Design«
Die Staatspreise von 1962 bis 2012

Harald Gruendl, Institute of Design Research Vienna (IDRV)

Die Geschichte des Staatspreises für »gute Form« 1962 beginnt an einem symbolträchtigen Ort – in der Wiener Secession, einer Institution, die von Vertretern der Wiener Moderne (u. a. Josef Hoffmann, Kolo Moser und Gustav Klimt) als Alternative zu dem zur Jahrhundertwende vorherrschenden konservativen, vom Historismus geprägten Kunstverständnis gegründet wurde. Und gerade dort veranstaltete das damals noch junge Österreichische Institut für Formgebung (ÖIF) die Ausstellung »Form = Qualität«. Die Ausstellung sollte beweisen, dass es trotz des damals wieder oder noch immer vorherrschenden Konservativismus im Österreich der Nachkriegszeit möglich war, »in Wien alle Geräte fürs tägliche Leben in einer unserem modernen Empfinden gemäßen Form zu kaufen« (»der Bau«, 4/1962). Die von Architekt und Designer Carl Auböck gestaltete Ausstellung zeigte unter anderem Gläser, Geschirr und Möbel, aber auch eine Aufzugkabine, Stoffe, Bestecke, eine Küche, Telefone und Radioapparate. Die Exponate waren aus am Markt erhältlichen, industriell hergestellten Waren ausgesucht worden. Es waren Beispiele der erfolgreichen Zusammenarbeit von Architekten, Entwerfern und Unternehmern, die ein ausgeprägter Qualitätssinn und die konsequente Suche nach der bis zu einem gewissen Grad auch ideologisierten »guten Form« vereinten. Das Bundesministerium für Handel und Wiederaufbau würdigte dieses Bestreben mit der Vergabe von Staatspreisen für »gute Form«. Eine Wasserwaage, ein Transistorradio, ein Kühlschrank und ein Besteck waren die ersten Preisträger im Rahmen einer vom österreichischen Staat unterstützten Förderung und Anerkennung der in Österreich noch jungen Disziplin »Industrial Design«. Das Zentrum der Volksbildung in Sachen Design und Architektur war das 1957 gegründete Österreichische Bauzentrum im Palais Liechtenstein in Wien. Und ebendort wurde 1965 das Zentrum Produktform – Design Centre eröffnet, ein ebenfalls von Carl Auböck entworfener 400 m² großer Ausstellungspavillon aus Betonfertigteilen im historischen Ambiente des Palais. Von da an wurde die »Österreichische Produktschau« in einer eigenen Ausstellungshalle gezeigt, und auch die nachfolgenden Staatspreise wurden in diesem Rahmen vergeben.

Die »13. Österreichische Produktschau« fand dann nach der Auflösung des Österreichischen Bauzentrums publikumswirksam in der Fußgängerzone Favoriten statt. Das Österreichische Institut für Formgebung bestand bis 1998, dann reichten die Mittel der Geldgeber nicht mehr aus, um den Betrieb aufrechtzuerhalten. So wurde nicht nur die jahrzehntelange Geschichte des Staatspreises unterbrochen, sondern auch die nationale und internationale Tätigkeit des ÖIF zur Förderung der Designpolitik eingestellt.

Seit 2001 wird der Preis im Zweijahresrhythmus wieder vergeben. designaustria, Interessenvertretung und Wissenszentrum für Design in Österreich, ist mit der Organisation des Preises betraut. Die Ausstellungen fanden zunächst im Looshaus statt; seit 2007 werden sie im designforum Wien im Wiener MuseumsQuartier gezeigt.

Ein Forschungsprojekt des Institute of Design Research Vienna hat nun die Aufgabe, die vollständige Liste der Preisträger und Preisträgerinnen zu recherchieren und damit ein wichtiges Kapitel der österreichischen Design- und Industriegeschichte, aber auch Alltags- und Kulturgeschichte zu dokumentieren. Als erstes Ergebnis dieses Forschungsprojekts wird nachstehend eine wissenschaftlich bearbeitete Liste der Staatspreisträger seit 1962 abgedruckt. Das Projekt könnte ohne die Koope-ration mit dem Museum für angewandte Kunst/ Gegenwartskunst (MAK) in Wien und designaustria nicht durchgeführt werden. Das MAK hat bereits die Staatspreise seit 1986 im Design-Info-Pool (dip), der virtuellen Sammlung österreichischen Designs des 20. und 21. Jahrhunderts, dokumentiert. Kunstsammlung und Archiv der Universität für angewandte Kunst Wien sind im Besitz des Bildnachlasses des ÖIF und haben die Forschungsarbeit ebenfalls unterstützt.

www.dip.mak.at

www.idrv.org

www.designaustria.at

http://sammlung.dieangewandte.at

From »Good Form« to »Design«
The National Design Prizes from 1962 to 2012

Harald Gruendl, Institute of Design Research Vienna (IDRV)

The history of the National Design Prize awarded for »Good Form« began in 1962 in a deeply symbolic place: at the Vienna Secession, an institution founded by the advocates of Viennese Modernism (Josef Hoffmann, Kolo Moser, Gustav Klimt, and others) as an alternative to the conservative understanding of art prevalent at the turn of the century, which at the time was still informed by Historicism. At this very place, the newly established Österreichisches Institut für Formgebung (ÖIF) organized the exhibition »Form = Quality«. The show was meant to prove that it was possible, in spite of the conservatism once again – or rather still – predominant in post-war Austria, »to purchase in Vienna all the appliances needed for daily life in a form corresponding to our modern spirit« (»der Bau«, 4/1962). The exhibition, conceived by the architect and designer Carl Auböck, presented, among other items, glassware, tableware, and furniture, but also a lift cabin, textiles, cutlery, a kitchen, telephones, and radio sets. The exhibits had been selected from industrially produced goods available on the market. They were highlighted as examples of successful collaborations between architects, designers, and business managers, all of whom shared a pronounced sense of quality and joined in a consistent search for »good form«, a concept that to some degree had also developed into an ideology. The Federal Ministry for Trade and Reconstruction honoured these efforts by awarding National Design Prizes for »Good Form«. A spirit level, a transistor radio, a refrigerator, and a cutlery set were the first winners chosen under the Austrian government's initiative to promote and recognize »industrial design«, then a still-young discipline in Austria. The hub of public education in design matters became the Österreichisches Bauzentrum, or Austrian Construction Centre, at the Liechtenstein Palace, founded in 1957. There, the Zentrum Produktform – Design Centre was opened in 1965: a 400-square-metre large exhibition pavilion of precast concrete elements likewise designed by Carl Auböck and integrated into the historical ambience of the palace. From then on, the »Austrian Product Show« was presented in its own exhibition hall, which also served as a venue for the subsequent award ceremonies of the National Design Prize.

When the Österreichisches Bauzentrum was finally closed down, the »13th Austrian Product Show« was held in the pedestrian zone in Favoriten, Vienna's tenth district, where it attracted a great deal of public attention. The Österreichisches Institut für Formgebung existed until 1998, when funds no longer sufficed to continue its operation. Thus not only was the decade-long history of the National Design Prize interrupted, but the national and international activities of the ÖIF directed at the implementation of a design policy also came to a halt.

The National Design Prize was resumed in 2001 and has been held every two years ever since, with designaustria, the interest organization and knowledge centre for design in Austria, entrusted with its realization. Initially the exhibitions were shown at the Looshaus; since 2007 they have been presented at the designforum Wien in the Vienna MuseumsQuartier.

It is now the task of a research project conducted by the Institute of Design Research Vienna to compile a complete list of the winners and thereby document an important chapter in the Austrian history of design, industry, everyday life, and culture. A first result of this project is the following list of the National Design Prize winners since 1962, which has been updated according to the latest findings. This project could not be realized without the support of the Austrian Museum of Applied Arts/Contemporary Art (MAK) in Vienna and designaustria. The MAK has documented the National Design Prizes from 1986 on in its Design Info Pool (dip), its virtual collection of Austrian design of the 20th and 21st centuries. The art collection and archives of the Vienna University of Applied Arts, preserving the picture archives of the former ÖIF, have also contributed to this project.

ÖIF-Ausstellung »Form = Qualität« in der Wiener Secession
ÖIF exhibition »Form = Quality« at the Vienna Secession

Staatspreis Design – Die Preisträger ab 1962
National Design Prize – The Winners as from 1962

1962–1986:	**Staatspreis für gute Form**
1987–1990:	**Staatspreis für gutes Design**
1991–1997:	**Staatspreis für Design**
ab 2001:	**Staatspreis Design**

Jahr Year	Preisträger Winner	Produkt Product	Auftraggeber & Produzent Client & Producer
1962	Hasso Gehrmann	Kühlschrank »de luxe«	Elektra Bregenz, Bregenz
	Eumig (WD)	Radio »Transistor 332«	Eumig Elekrtrizitäts- und Metallwarenindustrie, Wien
	Carl Auböck	Besteck »Modell 2080«	Neuzeughammer Ambosswerk, Wien
	Guido Scheyer	Wasserwaage »Sola AP«	Ing. Guido Scheyer, Götzis
	Carl Auböck	Service »Burg«	Tiroler Glashütte, Claus Josef Riedel KG, Kufstein
1963	Walter Grabner (WD)	Küche	Walter Grabner, Wien
1964	Svoboda & Co (WD)	Arbeitstisch »D 22«	Möbelwerk Svoboda & Co, St. Pölten
1965	Adele List	Hüte	Adele List, Wien
	Ch. Demel's Söhne (WD)	Zuckerwaren	Ch. Demel's Söhne, Zuckerbäcker, Wien
	J. & L. Lobmeyr Glaswaren	Kristallblock mit eingeschliffener Kugelkalotte	J. & L. Lobmeyr Glaswaren, Wien
1966[1]	Karl und Herma Kotal	Kinderzimmermöbel	Wiener Spielzeugschachtel, Wien
1967	Ernst W. Beranek	Toastgrill	Dr. Konrad Burg, Wien
	Max Schmid	Kunststoffverpackung für Geigy	Alpla-Werke, Alwin Lehner OHG, Hard
1968	Steyr-Daimler-Puch AG (WD)	Geländewagen »Haflinger 700 AP«	Steyr-Daimler-Puch AG, Wien
1969[1]	Reinhold Zwerger	Filmprojektor »Eumig Mark S-712«	Eumig Elekrtrizitäts- und Metallwarenindustrie, Wien
	Egon Rainer	Sitzmöbelprogramm	Pirmoser, Kufstein
1970	Helmuth Ohnmacht	Polybiwak, Biwagschachtel im Baukastensystem	Anton Fritz, Innsbruck
1971	Roman Czernik	Fertigteiltrafostation	Bauunternehmung und Betonwerk Dipl. Ing. Markus Papst, Frohnleiten
1972	Vereinigte Edelstahlwerke AG (WD)	Abbruchhammer B 220/II	Vereinigte Edelstahlwerke AG, Gebrüder Böhler & Co AG, Kapfenberg

Jahr Year	Preisträger Winner	Produkt Product	Auftraggeber & Produzent Client & Producer
1973	Reinhold Zwerger	Videokamera »Eumig VC 551«	Eumig Elektrizitäts- und Metallwarenindustrie, Wien
1974	Gernot Grabherr	Büromöbel-Organisationsprogramm	Bene Büromöbel KG, Waidhofen/Ybbs
1975	Werner Hölbl	Schichtenfilter »Ariston«	Theo Seitz Kellereimaschinen, Wien
1976	Ernst Beranek, Ulrich Dumpf	Hammerzange	Stubai Werkzeugindustrie Reg. Gen. mbH, Fulpmes
	Reinhold Zwerger	Kamerareihe »800«	Eumig Elektrizitäts- und Metallwaren-industrie, Wiener Neudorf
1977	Werner Hölbl	Ultramikrotom »Ultracut	C. Reichert Optische Werke AG, Wien
	Vereinigte Edelstahlwerke AG (WD)	Abbruchhammer »B 180«, Meißelhämmer »MH 41«, »MH 51«, »MH 61«	Vereinigte Edelstahlwerke AG, Wien
1978	I. D.-Pool (Ernst Beranek, Harald Kubelka, Dietmar Valentinitsch)	Blutgasanalysator »Gas-Check-940«	AVL – Abt. Elektromedizin, Graz
	Rudolf Svoboda	Transportable Dolmetscherkabine	SVOENT Svoboda Entwicklungs KG, St. Pölten
1979	I. D.-Pool (Ernst Beranek, Harald Kubelka, Dietmar Valentinitsch)	Myocard-Check »AVL 970«	AVL – Prof. List Gesellschaft mbH, Graz
	Porsche Design (Scholp, Mayersbeer)	Plotter »Servogor 281«	Goerz Electro Gesellschaft mbH, Wien
	Werner Hölbl	Feldstecher »Habicht SL«	Swarovski Optik KG, Solbad Hall
1980	Norbert Kotz	Brückenleuchte »Neue Wiener Reichsbrücke« (Projekt »Johann Nestroy«)	Austria Email AG, Wien
	Theodor Puschkarski	Verbindungselemente »Klem«	Klem System Austria Display + Messebau, Puschkarski GmbH, Wien
	Johann Svoboda	Arbeitsplatzkombination aus Programm »U 08«	Möbelwerk Svoboda & Co, St. Pölten
1981	Matthias Peschke	Armatur »Artweger Hard-Top Puch G«	Artweger-Industrie GmbH, Windischgarsten
	Design-Büro Hartmann	Universalkessel Typ »VarioLyt«	Hoval-Werk für Heizungstechnik GmbH, Marchtrenk

Jahr Year	Preisträger Winner	Produkt Product	Auftraggeber & Produzent Client & Producer
1981	Franz Drbal	U-Bahn-Doppeltriebwagen »Wien«	Simmering-Graz-Pauker AG, Wien
1982	Ioan Kloss, Karl-Heinz Krug	Holzbearbeitungsmaschine »Emcostar 2000 Universal«	Emco Maier & Co Fabrik für Spezialmaschinen, Hallein
1983	Udo Geißler	Osram-Diabetrachter »Diastar 251 A«	Osram – Österreichische Glühlampenfabrik GmbH, Wien
1984	James G. Skone	Reibungskletterschuh »Super Magic«	Salewa GmbH Österreich, Salzburg
	Dietmar Valentinitsch	Ultraschall-Diagnostikgerät »Combison 320«	Kretztechnik GmbH, Zipf
1985	Gerhard Heufler, Wolfgang Gsöll	Kabelhalterung für Fassaden »KABFA«	Mosdorfer GmbH, Weiz
	Gerhard Heufler	Notsender/Ortungsgerät für Lawinenverschüttete und Thermotasche »Pieps DF«	Motronic Elektronische Geräte GmbH, Groß St. Florian
	Alfred Seidl	Glasserie »Anatol«	Stölzle Kristall GmbH, Wien
1986	Porsche Design	A3-Grafikplotter »SE 283«	Goerz Electro GmbH, Wien
	Wilh. Grundmann GmbH (WD)	Behindertenbeschlagsgarnitur »GEOS 1754/D6/5«	Wilh. Grundmann GmbH, Rohrbach-Gölsern
	Valentinitsch Design	Kunststoff-Spritzgießmaschine »BA 350«	Battenfeld Austria, Kottingbrunn
1987	Christian Ploderer, Theodor Puschkarski	Halogen-Wandstrahler »KlemLite°«	Klem-System International, Puscharski GmbH, Wien
	I. D.-Pool (Ernst Beranek, Harald Kubelka)	Etagenkessel »KSN« für feste Brennstoffe Seekirchen	Windhager Zentralheizung GmbH,
	Johannes Stadler	Windsurfsegel »NPU Speed Wing«	NPU, Oberwölz
1988	Peschke + Skone	Miniaturmikrofon »C 409«	AKG Akustische und Kino-Geräte GmbH, Wien
	Haus-Rucker-Co, Laurids Ortner Industrial Design Company	Büroeinrichtungsprogramm »C 5«	Bene Büromöbel KG, Waidhofen/Ybbs
	Krug & Kloss	Holzbearbeitungsmaschine »Woodworker«	Emco Maier & Co, Hallein
1989	Manfred Lechner	Motormäher »Jet Neu«	Vogel & Noot GmbH, Wartberg
	Peschke + Skone	Kopfhörer »K 1000«	AKG Akustische und Kino-Geräte GmbH, Wien

Jahr Year	Preisträger Winner	Produkt Product	Auftraggeber & Produzent Client & Producer
1989	Schlagheck und Schultes	Alpinskibindung »VAR Racing«	Atomic GmbH, Wagrain
1990	Peschke + Skone	Blut- und Infusionswärmer »BW 385«	Ernst Biegler GmbH, Mauerbach
	Steyr-Landmaschinen-technik GmbH (WD)	Traktorkabine »SK2«	Steyr-Landmaschinentechnik GmbH, St. Valentin
	Helmut Jörg, Rudolf Kamenik	Schneckengetriebe mit Ventilator »Unice«	Louis Jörg GmbH, Wien
	Leslie L. Lane	Schalen und Vase »Vulcano«	Oberglas-Bärnbach GmbH, Bärnbach
1991	Christian Fenzl, Peter Scheer	Löschfahrzeug »Panther 8 x 8«	Rosenbauer AG, Leonding
1992	Werner Hölbl	Fernglas »Habicht SLC«	Swarovski Optik, Absam
	Gerhard Heufler	Kompostwendemaschine »Topturn 3000«	Komptech GmbH, Graz
	Valentinitsch Design	Durchflussregler Serie »101«	Wittmann Kunststoffgeräte GmbH, Wien
1993	Karin Pesau	Leuchte »Mildes Licht RCA«	Zumtobel Lighting GmbH, Dornbirn
	Kiska Industrial Design	Überflurhydrant	MKE, Heidenreichstein
	S.YN = Design GmbH (Reinhard Hansen, Leon Widdison)	Messepräsentationssytem »System Case«	Expo Norm, Salzburg
1994	Helmut Link	Katamaran »Linkat«	Link, Wien
1995	Gerhard Heufler	Schienenfräsmaschine »DHE 675«	Jenbacher Energiesysteme AG, Jenbach
1996	Kiska Industrial Design	Kooperation Skidata – Kiska	Skidata Computer GmbH, Gartenau
1997	Gerhard Heufler	Minensuchgerät »Mimid Miniatur Mine Detector«	Schiebel Elektronische Geräte GmbH, Wien
2001	Zeug Design GmbH (Erwin Weitgasser, Detlev Magerer)	Kickboards »kick two«, »carve two«	K2 Ski-, Sport- und Mode GmbH, Penzberg, Deutschland (AG); Playmaker, Taichung, Taiwan (P)
2003	**Konsumgüter:**		
	EOOS Design GmbH	Stuhl »Sweet Wood«	Montina S.R.L., Udine, Italien
	Investitionsgüter:		
	Kiska Design	AVL Product Design	AVL List GmbH, Graz

Jahr Year	Preisträger Winner	Produkt Product	Auftraggeber & Produzent Client & Producer
2005	**Konsumgüter :**		
	René Chavanne	Tragbares Eventmöbel »JustinCase«	JustinCase.at und diverse Partner, Wien
	Investitionsgüter:		
	Gerhard Heufler	Unbemannter Helikopter »Camcopter® S-100«	Schiebel Elektronische Geräte GmbH, Wien
	Räumliche Gestaltung:		
	PPAG (Anna Popelka, Georg Poduschka)	Hofmöblierung MuseumsQuartier Wien »Enzi«	MuseumsQuartier Errichtungs- und Betriebsgmbh, Wien (AG); PPAG, Wien und diverse Partner (P)
2007	**Konsumgüter:**		
	mikimartinek	Wein- und Wassergläser »Achtel« und »Europe«	ÖVGW, Lebensministerium (AG); J. & L. Lobmeyr, Wien (P)
	Investitionsgüter:		
	breuerbono design consulting; Walch GmbH (Christian Walch, Andreas Moll, Dietmar Kohler)	Fenster- und Fassadensystem »Walchfenster 04«	Walch GmbH, Ludesch
	Räumliche Gestaltung:		
	memux (Thomas Mennel, Reinhard Muxel)	Betonvorhang	Oberhauser & Schedler Bau GmbH, Andelsbuch (Prototyp)
2009	**Konsumgüter:**		
	Peter Kuschnigg, Otto Bock Healthcare Products (WD)	Handprothese »Axon Hand System«	Otto Bock Healthcare Products GmbH, Wien
	Investitionsgüter:		
	GP designpartners gmbh	Solarleuchte »Champ«	HEI Consulting GmbH, Wien
	Räumliche Gestaltung:		
	Oskar Leo Kaufmann & Albert Rüf Ziviltechniker GmbH	Bausystem »System3«	The Museum of Modern Art, New York, USA (AG); Kaufmann Zimmerei und Tischlerei, Reuthe (P)

Jahr Year	Preisträger Winner	Produkt Product	Auftraggeber & Produzent Client & Producer
2011	**Konsumgüter:**		
	Thomas Feichtner	Stauraumsystem »Ego«	Franz Blaha Sitz- und Büromöbel Industrie GmbH, Korneuburg
	Investitionsgüter:		
	formquadrat gmbh	Großwasserenthärter »Rondomat Duo S«	BWT Aktiengesellschaft, Mondsee
	Räumliche Gestaltung:		
	Isa Stein Studio für Kunst und Architektur (Isa Stein, Christoph Fürst)	Sprache als Umsetzung des Themas Integration	Stiftung St. Severin, Linz (AG); Isa Stein Studio für Kunst und Architektur, Linz, und diverse Partner (P)

[1] In diesen beiden Jahren wurde der Staatspreis für gute Form zweimal ausgeschrieben, wobei er jedoch 1966 nur einmal zur Vergabe kam; das andere Mal wurden lediglich Ehrenpreise vergeben.

Abkürzungen . Abbreviations
AG = Auftraggeber . Client
P = Produzent . Producer
WD = Werkdesign . In-house design

Redaktion . Editorial supervision
Ulrike Haele – IDRV

Recherche . Research
Heidi Caltik – MAK, Design-Info-Pool (dip)
Harald Gruendl, Ulrike Haele, Lotte Kristoferitsch, Ronja Ulrich – IDRV
Severin Filek – designaustria
Silvia Herkt – Universität für angewandte Kunst Wien, Kunstsammlung und Archiv

Impressum . Publisher's Information

AMBRA |V

© 2013 AMBRA | V (und Autoren . and authors)
AMBRA | V is part of Medecco Holding GmbH, Vienna

Herausgeber . Edited by
designaustria (DA), Wissenszentrum und Interessenvertretung, www.designaustria.at
Bundesministerium für Wirtschaft, Familie und Jugend, www.bmwfj.gv.at
Austria Wirtschaftsservice GmbH, www.awsg.at

Redaktion . Editors
Brigitte Willinger, Severin Filek, designaustria, Wien

Übersetzung . Translation
Brigitte Willinger, Wien

Lektorat . Copy-text Editing
Brigitte Willinger, Wien (Deutsch . German)
Edita Nosowa, Minneapolis (Englisch . English)

Gestaltung . Design
Robert Sabolovic, Johanna Philipp, zeitmass, Wien

Trophäengestaltung . Trophy Design
Klemens Kubala

Fotos . Photo Credits
Alle Rechte liegen bei den Einreichern und Beitragenden bzw. deren Fotografen.
All rights reserved by the entrants, contributors, and their photographers.
Namentlich genannt wurden . Mentioned by name were
BMWFJ/Ernst Kainerstorfer (Reinhold Mitterlehner), FBI Photography (Tèo), Monika Nguyen (Perfekt Box), Sigrid Rauchdobler (Pixel im Turm), David Schreyer, Eric Sidoroff (Ich lasse mich nicht länger für einen Narren halten), Daniel George (Fritz Frenkler), Florian Lehmann (Mute), Studio Messlinger (Widefrigde, Frischhalten), Croce & Wir (Stefanie Grüssl und Trophäe Staatspreis Design), Irina Gavrich (Sabine Pümpel), Carl Auböck Archiv (ÖIF-Ausstellung)

Papier . Paper
Olin Regular absolute white 150 g/m², zur Verfügung gestellt von . supplied by
Antalis Austria GmbH, Wien
Gedruckt auf säurefreiem, chlorfrei gebleichtem Papier – TCF-zertifiziert
Printed on acid-free and chlorine-free bleached paper – TCF-certified

Druck und Verarbeitung . Produced and Printed by
Die Stadtdrucker, Wien

Erste Auflage . First edition
ISBN 978-3-99043-601-1   AMBRA | V
Printed in Austria

Ausstellung . Exhibition
designforum Wien, Museumsplatz 1, 1070 Wien
25. September bis 10. November 2013 . 25 September to 10 November 2013

Ausstellungsgestaltung . Exhibition Design
Heidi Resch, designaustria, und Thomas Hamann, Wien

Durchführung . Organization
designaustria: Severin Filek, Heidi Resch, Verena Reindl, Brigitte Willinger, Ulrike Willinger
Bundesministerium für Wirtschaft, Familie und Jugend: Stefanie Grüssl, Dieter Böhm
Austria Wirtschaftsservice GmbH: Sabine Pümpel

Ihr Partner für Papier und Umwelt

Intakte Umwelt ist ein erlesenes Gut. Sie ist der Stoff aus dem die Zukunft schöpft. Antalis ist sich dieser partnerschaftlichen Verantwortung bewusst. Deshalb fördern wir den Verkauf von Recyclingpapieren und Papieren aus nachhaltiger Forstwirtschaft. Dokumentiert wird dies unter anderem durch die Zertifizierung von Antalis bei den bedeutenden Zertifizierungssystemen FSC und PEFC. Wenn Sie mehr zu unserem Sortiment erfahren wollen kontaktieren Sie unsere Verkaufsteams in Wien, Linz oder in Innsbruck.

Papier ist wiederverwertbar und unterstützt eine nachhaltige Forstwirtschaft. Papier ist weiterhin das meistgenutzte Kommunikationsmittel der Welt.